"It's Time You Believe"

Becky,

Thank you for pouring into my life!

Love,
Chrissie Guy

"It's Time You Believe"

The Voice That Changed My Life

Chrissie Cory

WestBow
PRESS
A DIVISION OF THOMAS NELSON

WestBow Press books may be ordered through booksellers or by contacting:

WestBow Press
A Division of Thomas Nelson
1663 Liberty Drive
Bloomington, IN 47403
www.westbowpress.com
1-(866) 928-1240

All Scripture quotations, unless otherwise indicated, are taken from THE AMPLIFIED BIBLE: OLD TESTAMENT. ©1962, 1964 by Zondervan (used by permission); and from THE AMPLIFIED BIBLE: NEW TESTAMENT. © 1958 by the Lockman Foundation (used by permission). Scripture quotations marked NIV1984 are from Holy Bible, New International Version ®, NIV ®. Copyright © 1973, 1978, 1984 by Biblica, Inc. Used by permission. All rights reserved worldwide. Scripture quotations marked NIV are from Holy Bible, New International Version ®, NIV ®. Copyright © 1973, 1978, 1984, 2011 by Biblica, Inc. Used by permission. All rights reserved worldwide. Scripture quotations marked NASB are from NEW AMERICAN STANDARD BIBLE®, © The Lockman Foundation 1960, 1962, 1963, 1968, 1971, 1972, 1973, 1975, 1977, 1995. Used by permission. Scripture quotations marked MSG from THE MESSAGE. Copyright © by Eugene H. Peterson 1993, 1994, 1995, 1996, 2000, 2001, 2002. Used by permission of NavPress Publishing Group.

ISBN: 978-1-4497-6836-2 (sc)
ISBN: 978-1-4497-6837-9 (hc)
ISBN: 978-1-4497-6835-5 (e)

Library of Congress Control Number: 2012917707

Printed in the United States of America
WestBow Press rev. date: 1/11/2013

Contents

Introduction

For years I searched for love, but instead I found heartbreak. Time passed without my even realizing that I was on a path of destruction. The unhealthy lifestyle I was stuck in only came to an end when I listened to the voice.

During my teen years, I made a series of poor choices based on lies I then believed, lies that affected several areas of my life. In hindsight I can see how the false beliefs I held, held me, how they blinded me from the truth and led me into difficult, if not dangerous, relationships. Becoming a parent and remembering my childhood as my own daughter's unfolded, I often had flashbacks of words I had said and attitudes I had developed along the way. Moments in my daughter's growing-up years reminded me of the poor choices I made and the huge mess that resulted. But the night I heard the voice, my life radically changed. I was twenty-three, depressed, lost, all too aware of the wasted years of my life, and regretting most of the decisions I had made, yet my life began to change.

When I started sharing my transformation as a testimony to God's grace and goodness, friends and family suggested I write a book about my experience. At first I laughed at the suggestion. "Me? Write a book? English was my worse subject in school!" I insisted. "Who am I to write a book?" The idea seemed daunting, twenty years passed, and then, at the age of forty-three, I sensed God telling me it was time for me to start writing. He knocked down each of my excuses one by one and even gave me a friend to help. It has taken many years of plugging along and overcoming obstacles, but I hope and pray that my story will encourage young women to make good decisions, to—if they're already headed in an unhealthy direction—leave behind that path of destruction and choose a path of peace and contentment. It isn't easy for me to share my horrid mistakes, and I am not at all proud of my past, but I want to lay out the whole truth and hold nothing back.

Dear readers, I pray that God will touch and bless you through my story.

Chrissie Cory

Chapter 1

My Not-So-Perfect World

Having just finished teaching my aerobics class on a muggy Florida evening, I jumped into the Trans Am convertible my boyfriend Tony had loaned me. With the top down, I raced toward our apartment, the wind blowing through my blonde hair. I felt on top of the world; life was good. After all, I had a handsome bodybuilder for a boyfriend, I had a good paying job at an elite health club, and, in tip-top shape, I looked fabulous. I'd dyed my hair platinum and tanned my skin a golden bronze. I might not be a Perfect Ten, but I was close enough to feel confident I could keep Tony loving me. That was the important thing.

The apartment we had shared for the past year had a view of the Intercoastal Waterway. Proud to be living in such a nice complex, admiring the pool, and enjoying the boats rocking against the dock, I held my head high as I drove in to park. I hurried inside the apartment, quickly showered, and redid my makeup and hair. Studying my reflection in the mirror to make sure I looked as pretty as possible, I hoped Tony would be pleased. I glanced at the clock and wondered where he was. He was late *again*. My stomach tightened. I wondered what his story would be this time.

"He'll be here soon," I told myself, going into the kitchen to prepare dinner. By the time the meal was ready, Tony still hadn't arrived. *Where was he?* Trying to relax, I lit a cigarette and fixed myself a diet coke with rum and lime before sitting down to wait. An hour passed before I heard the key turn in the lock. I breathed a sigh of relief. He was finally home! I ran to him and jumped into his arms, wrapping my legs around him.

"Hey, babe, I got something special for you," Tony said as he reached into his pocket.

My heart was pounding. *Maybe this would be the ring I'd been waiting for.* He smiled and pulled out a tiny jar of white powder, cocaine to spice up the evening.

At least he's thinking of me and wanting us to have a good time together, I told myself, hiding my disappointment. At the age of twenty-two, I thought I had it all, but little did I know, my world was about to crumble.

When I was growing up, I didn't say to myself, "One day I'd like to be a drug addict." No, I had the same dreams most girls have. I hoped to meet my soul mate and live happily ever after. I pictured myself having a beautiful home, fancy cars, and traveling the world. And I was convinced that, with Tony, all my dreams would come true. Unfortunately my life turned into a nightmare. As I've thought back over those years, I often wondered how—in my search for love and happiness—I got on such a destructive path and why I kept traveling it.

I was born the day before President John F. Kennedy was assassinated. As the nurse presented me to my mother for the first time, she also shared that awful news. In her shock, my mother almost dropped me. So my life began.

Apparently I cried a lot when I was little and grew into a strong-willed child. When I was a baby, my constant fussing distressed my mother. Frustrated with my tears, she would shake her head and appreciate the fact that at least her other daughter (my sister who was five years older than me) had never cried so much. I was the difficult child, stubborn and easily angered, and my sister was the angel, born with a halo over her head.

As I grew older, I heard my mother complain to her friends about me, telling them I had cried from the time I was born until I was eight years old. "I sometimes have to go and sit in the car to escape," she would say. As I got older, having heard over and over how much of a bother I was as a baby, I began to think my mother didn't like me very much. I asked her once if I had done anything right when I was little. She shrugged and said, "Well, you were a pretty baby." At least I had my looks going for me, but apparently not much else.

Unfortunately, my sister wasn't too happy to have me join the family either. She was aggravated with all the energy it took to keep me happy. I made my parents tired, and they didn't have the strength to play with her as they once had. Upset that her needs weren't being met, my sister blamed me. Just a child trying to figure out why her world had changed so drastically, she directed her anger toward me, the intruder who had invaded her life. She would, for instance, bite her arm and then run up to my mother with tears in her eyes. "Mommy, look what Chrissie did," she whined, hoping to convince my mother to take me back to wherever I had come from. When she realized that tactic didn't work, she tried other ways to divert attention from me to herself. I don't blame her. She was hurting and felt unimportant and unloved. If our roles had been reversed, I probably would have acted the same way.

Having an older sister who didn't like me definitely made life more difficult for me. Not a day went by when she wouldn't taunt me until I exploded and charged at her in rage, my face hot and red. I wanted to hit her, hurt her, but instead she laughed in my face. She got great pleasure from this activity, but I would feel completely defeated emotionally and physically, I would retreat to my bedroom. Thank God I had my own room!

I will never forget one summer day when I was playing in the front yard. I heard the van that sprayed for mosquitoes coming toward our house. I tried to run inside for shelter, but my sister and her friend locked me out, taunting through the window, "You're gonna die! You're gonna die!" I banged on the door, wailing for them to let me in. As the van came nearer, I thought that, at the tender age of seven, I was about to breathe my last. *Oh my God, my sister hates me this much?* At that point, I realized I could not trust my sister. Years later she still laughed about that incident, but for a long time I had nightmares over it.

As the two of us grew older, our differences showed up more and more in both our looks and personalities. We grew further apart as time went by, and her resentment toward me continued to grow. Thankfully, we were far enough apart in age that we didn't have to attend the same school. While I was in middle school, she was in high school, but our arguments and hurtful comments continued at home. In high school I remember dressing for dates and my sister commenting unfavorably about my outfits. She had a good eye for fashion, and her remarks stung, shattering my confidence. It would have been nice for her to encourage me and offer tips on how to dress and wear make-up. Instead, not only did she make me feel like a hopeless project, but she also seemed to enjoy pointing out my flaws. As I got older, I became wiser about handling her wrath—and avoiding it. I would sneak into her room while she was out, use her makeup, and even wear her clothes. But when she was home, I stayed out of her way and never talked to her about anything. We lived two very separate lives.

While we were growing up, our parents worked hard to have us avoid sibling rivalry and minimize the obvious strife between my sister and me. Mom and Dad, for instance, rarely gave either my sister or me compliments or spoke words of encouragement. I can't remember them ever saying, "Great job!" or "Well done" about anything I did when I was growing up. I guess my parents hoped that not complimenting either of us on our individual strengths would somehow help the two of us get along.

Yet when it came to discipline, my parents treated us as equals. If one of us needed a spanking, both of us received one. They didn't take sides or choose to blame one of us over the other. Instead, we were both wrong. I know that my parents tried to be fair and that babies don't come out of the womb with parenting handbooks, but their parenting method completely backfired. Furthermore, my mother would talk about our differences to family and friends. She always explained how opposite my sister and I were. As we grew up, my sister and I competed more and more with each other, and we ended up disliking one another intensely.

My mother, busy pursuing her own dreams was no help in the situation with my sister: she was never an ally or protector. Then, when I started grade school, she went back to college and spent a lot of time studying. Usually my mom was home physically when I returned from school, but she was not there emotionally. And then one time she wasn't physically where I needed her....

—⌒—

I will never forget the afternoon when I was in third grade and a terrible storm struck just as school was being let out. I lived only a couple blocks from school, and I usually walked home. But on this afternoon the clouds were dark, and hail the size of quarters was falling from the sky. Rows of cars were lined up along the street. Moms were there ready to pick up their kids, but my mother was nowhere in sight. I tried to run for it, but the rain and hail beating down on me made it impossible for me to even see where I was going. Feeling helpless, I asked one of the moms to give me a ride. My mother finally showed up at home thirty minutes after I arrived home safely. She said that she'd been at the school but must have missed me.... It never failed. My mom was always late, her mind was on other things, and she just moved at a different pace than I did, so I gave up on ever depending on her.

She tried to be a good mother, but it didn't help that we have completely opposite personalities. She loved to read; I hated books. She liked me to wear dresses; I gagged at the thought of wearing anything she suggested. By the time I was in middle school, Mom stopped making suggestions. Stressed out and not having much of a support system since my father traveled constantly with his work, she allowed me to do whatever I wanted without comment. Having been raised by an overprotective, hovering mother herself, she was determined to not be that way. Though part of me liked the independent lifestyle she gave me, another part of me felt as if I didn't really fit in with my family. I felt as if I were too much of a problem for her to deal with. Though we loved each other, we had trouble showing it. We rarely gave each other hugs or spoke any words of affection. Bottom line, we didn't have much of a relationship at all. My dad and I were more alike, but every week he was gone from Monday through Friday and home only on Saturday and Sunday.

But I do have some fond memories from my childhood. I loved playing with my dog and watching my dad train him. (He had trained German shepherds in the army, so our dog was very well behaved.) Going to the college football and basketball games on weekends, riding on my dad's shoulders, and cheering for our home team—those were also good times.

But unfortunately, since we were so much alike, my dad and I often butted heads. Our tempers would flare whenever the both of us were set in our ways and neither one of us was willing to budge.

At other times, my dad—who grew up in a poor home—shared sad stories from his painful childhood. His alcoholic father tended to call him a stupid, dumb kid. My father had to wear clothes bought at the local thrift store. One day at school he was thoroughly humiliated when someone noticed my dad wearing clothes he had once worn. My father took a huge step forward in life by successfully providing for us and giving us a much better home life than the one he had experienced. He worked hard during the week and he was always home with us on the weekends.

But, sadly, on the weekends, I found myself afraid of my father's unpredictable rage. In the mornings, he usually was in a good mood, but as the day progressed, he'd grow tired and irritable, showing his powerful temper. He never became physically violent with any of us, but his ranting about little things made both my sister and me jumpy. I never could understand what set him off, so I often felt as though I was walking on a minefield. I never knew when a bomb would go off.

And God forbid if I broke anything when he was around. My father would get so angry so fast and scream about how I'd screwed up. He also got frustrated with my sister and me if we didn't do a specific task correctly. He would be extremely aggravated and end up doing it himself. The more he yelled, the more nervous we became--and the more unable to concentrate on the assigned chore. As I got older, I was fearful of the unknown, of not knowing how he would react. Would he be calm and reasonable, or would he scream and yell? Eventually I learned to avoid my father as much as I could.

To outsiders, though—to people who didn't see his dark side—my dad had a great personality and was a real comedian. Too often to count he would have relatives and friends rolling on the floor with uncontrollable laughter. But on some occasions his joking hurt my feelings. At first I laughed at his humor, but then my laughter turned to internal tears as a result of a cutting remark he would make. One Christmas I received two bottles of perfume as gifts, and he remarked, "People must think you stink pretty bad to get you perfume." Everyone laughed, but I wanted to punch him in the face.

I believe my father loved me and wanted the best for me, but just didn't know how to show it. Desiring to make me a better person, he tended to focus on my flaws, causing me to feel inadequate. His harping on my negative qualities far outweighed any positive things he said. It was difficult to receive his love and encouragement in the midst of all his negativity and so-called humor. He would point out the huge blemish on my face and the ugly eyeliner I was wearing or comment that I was eating too much and would get fat. My father's words were tearing me down, bit by bit. Very aware of my own flaws, I started working to improve them so just maybe he wouldn't find anything negative to say. But he always found something to complain about—and he never hesitated to point it out. Frustrated that I could never measure up to his expectations. With a mean and perhaps jealous sister, a distant mother, and a negative father, I looked elsewhere for love and acceptance.

Clearly, my home wasn't exactly a haven I could turn to for comfort. Spending time with friends I had known since kindergarten became more enjoyable for me than spending time with my own family. But to my surprise, when I was in sixth grade, a couple of classmates turned against me. They started calling me "Prissy Chrissie," and they mimicked the way I walked and talked. One girl would flip her hand out in a prissy way, repeating words I had said. Those around her laughed, and I felt humiliated and very self-conscious. I was devastated. I had no idea what I had done to deserve their unkind treatment. I was just being myself, but just like at home, that wasn't good enough for these girls either. Something must be wrong with me. Why else would they continue to torment me?

Unfortunately, during this time I was going through puberty, and for me that meant bad acne. One day a boy in my class loudly asked me if I had the chicken pox. When several students turned to stare, my face turned bright red. I wanted to crawl under my desk and hide. I felt totally alone, and inside I was dying. After feeling ridiculed at home, the last thing I needed was to get the same treatment at school.

All this led me to make certain conclusions. I came to believe that looking good and being accepted by my peers was critical for my survival. I was also convinced that if I could be perfect in every way, I would finally be happy.

Chapter 2

Looking for Love

By the end of that horrible school year, I was very motivated to change my image before going on to seventh grade. Middle school would be a fresh new start for me. So that summer I studied the popular girls— how they dressed, how they talked, how they wore their hair, how they acted. I noticed that several of them smoked cigarettes. Well, if that's what it takes, I'd smoke too. My friend and I got some cigarettes from her older brother, and we hid behind a truck to light one up. It made me sick at first and I almost lost my lunch, but I was determined. Desperately wanting to fit in, I imitated those girls I admired, and by the end of the summer, I not only looked like them, but I also smoked like a pro. When school started, I was thrilled to see that I had no trouble being accepted by the smoking crowd.

Thinking it would make me even more cool, I shortened my name to Chris. As I made changes like that, the people around me took notice and accepted me into their cliques. I was finding new friends, and I was ignoring my friends from sixth grade, who weren't making any necessary adjustments to fit in. To this day I feel bad about how I treated them. I'm sure they wondered what they did wrong. They didn't do anything wrong, but I was in the cool group now and I wanted to stay there. Hanging with the unpopular crowd was too much of a risk for me. I couldn't survive another year of being "Prissy Chrissie."

Still feeling insecure and self-conscious about my flaws, I went to work on my complexion, knowing it didn't compare to the popular girls. I went to a dermatologist, and the medicine he gave me helped some… but not enough. Of course one rude seventh-grade boy had to remind me of that fact. Pushing me up against the locker, he yelled in my face that I'd be pretty if I didn't have all those zits. He totally crushed the little self-esteem I had…. At that point, I aggressively tried every over-the-counter product out there to clear up my skin, but I had the greatest success with just piling on makeup. One day that boy would regret he ever said that to me—and that day did come!

By eighth grade I had made it onto the cheerleading squad, a new level of popularity, and my social circle grew. Nothing feels better than walking down the halls wearing a cheerleading uniform, having everyone admire you, and just wanting that boy who called me "zit face" to take a look at me now. I was feeling mighty special because I was finally part of the universally popular crowd. In fact, I was part of two groups that started to merge. I gladly included my smoking buddies, who started experimenting with drugs when they entered this new circle. Once smoking a cigarette was cool; now smoking pot was the key to cool. It was a natural progression for them, and where was I? I spent time with the popular girls who played around with drug use, but I walked to school with kids who used heavily. I was in the middle, but partying with drugs and alcohol had definitely become one of my favorite recreational activities: I'd sneak alcohol out of my parents' liquor cabinet, and my friends and I would spike our drinks and laugh uncontrollably until we almost peed our pants. On weekends a group of us would get high, walk to the mall, or go see a movie. I spent most Friday nights at a girlfriend's, staying up late partying, unsupervised by adults. My parents would have died if they'd known, but they trusted me and suspected absolutely nothing.

Looking back at that time of my life, I honestly don't know how I managed to get through. Smoking a joint was often part of my morning ritual as I walked to school, so I was in a daze many times during first period. But I didn't care much about my education. My grades suffered, but so what? My social life flourished, and that meant more to me. Why would I care about my grades when everyone knew my name and boys began to notice me?

I was finally happy, and I was confident that my high school years would only be better. Until one evening, my parents told me about their plans to move south to Florida. At first I was reluctant, but to have summer weather all year round—that just might be a dream come true.

But it turned into a nightmare.

Before I knew it, we had sold our house and everything we owned. I was fifteen years old and moving to the unknown with my mother, a recent college graduate, and my father, who wanted a career change and had hopes of living a better life. My sister was attending the local college, so she stayed back to finish her degree. Excited about the move, I thought the South would be just like Iowa except better because we wouldn't have to fight the snow.

That June we settled in, renting a condo near the beach on the southern tip of Florida. After the long summer of bathing in the sun, reality hit me hard: I found out that the high school I would be attending was much worse—in many ways—than I had ever imagined. In Iowa, for instance, the high school I would have attended had an indoor pool, a basketball auditorium, a theater, and a huge football field. Despite the wealth of the city, the Florida high school had none of these amenities, nor did it seem to have much school spirit. Instead, the majority of the kids did drugs, skipped school, and hung out at the beach all day long instead of being at all involved in team sports. This was a major culture shock for me.

Furthermore, the Florida city we'd moved to happened to be one of the richest in the United States, and my middle-class family stuck out like a rundown Volkswagen in a parking lot full of shiny Cadillacs. The kids at this school drove fancy cars, not the junked-up, hand-me-downs I had seen back in Iowa. Their vehicles were brand-new, right off the dealership lot. Of course I admired the popular, rich, perfectly polished, bleached-blonde girls who drove their expensive cars and dressed in their designer outfits. Their world seemed absolutely perfect, and I dreamed that I would one day be as rich as they were. In the meantime, I walked through the halls thinking I was turning the pages and looking at the pictures of a glamour magazine. I never knew teenagers could live this way. It was as if I had moved to a different country.

———

During the entire first week of school, only one girl spoke to me. She said, with a smug expression on her face, "You're not from around here, are you?" Looking at me with pity, she clearly let me know that I needed to work on my image. Whenever I said I was from Iowa, these Florida folks would glare at me and ask, "Where's that?" as if they had never heard of the state. This transition from being one of the most popular girls in my school to being an invisible stranger, where no one noticed me, was a crushing blow. I couldn't believe this was happening to me. On the days when no one even said a word to me, the pain was overwhelming, and I had a hard time holding back the tears.

Weeks went by.... Eventually I met a girl named Tracy, who was outgoing, but not particularly popular. I felt sorry for her. She thought everyone loved her, but behind her back, people tended to make fun of her. She struck up a conversation with me during our English class, and, desperate for a friend, I was thankful to have her even though her pushiness and incessant chatter tended to get on my nerves.

One day she announced that I should go to homecoming with a senior named Carl, who was a good friend of the boy she dated. Since I didn't know this boy at all, I felt very uneasy, especially since he was much older than I was. I told Tracy in no uncertain terms that I didn't want to go, but she kept pushing me, begging me to at least talk to him on the phone. Not feeling particularly good about it, I finally agreed and gave her my phone number. Anything to stop her nagging!

That evening Carl called, and we actually talked for a couple hours. I was really nervous—and very thankful that our first meeting was over the phone and not in person. Carl seemed nice and genuinely interested in getting to know me, and that helped me relax a little bit. As the conversation ended, we agreed to meet during lunch at school the next day.

I could barely eat anything at lunch. My nerves were back in full force, and they definitely had the best of me. I barely made eye contact with Carl because I was expecting him to reject me, but instead he made a real effort to impress me. All week long he walked me to class, and in the evenings he would call. After much persuasion I agreed to go to the homecoming dance with him. He was thrilled—and I was scared to death. I couldn't get past the fact that Carl was a senior and I was only a freshman. I had never dated anyone older before. I was nervous, inexperienced, and afraid I would screw this up.

I was grateful to learn that Carl and I would be going with another couple. Double-dating would make homecoming a lot less uncomfortable for me! At least that's what I thought, but I was so nervous at dinner! I accepted the beer when it was offered, and it went straight to my head. We spent twenty minutes at the dance, got our picture taken, had one slow dance, and left. To be honest, prom night was a big blur for me, but prom was the first date of many. We would go to dinner and the movies, but most of the time we would drink beer, smoke a joint, and hang out at some local party. The alcohol calmed my nerves. When I felt more relaxed, I could enjoy myself instead of worrying about messing up and not measuring up to my peers. At the time I thought the alcohol helped me, but in retrospect I can see how it clouded my judgment.

After we had dated for several months, Carl began pressuring me to have sex. I was really freaked out about the whole thing. I was afraid my parents would find out or—worse—I would end up pregnant. I wasn't ready to take that big step, but Carl was. He had been sexually active with his last girlfriend and was trying to be patient with me, but I sensed he was getting sick of my saying no. I didn't want to lose him because he was the only friend I had—and what kind of social life would I have without him? I didn't want to think about it. I just hoped the problem would go away.

One evening Carl took me to his house to watch a movie. We walked in the door and got comfortable on the couch. As the night went on, we had quite a buzz from drinking beer, and we topped it off a few hits from a joint. His parents were out, and we had the whole house to ourselves. Before I knew it, he was yelling at me from the top of the stairs to come up to his bedroom. I stumbled up the stairs, and as I approached his room, he grabbed me and threw me down on the bed. We started our typical make-out session, but soon he was overpowering me to do more than what I felt comfortable doing. Intoxicated, tired, thinking my boyfriend was out of control, and feeling trapped, I gave in. Right after Carl had gotten what he wanted, he heard his folks drive up. He dropped me and raced to get dressed. I stumbled to the floor and made my way to the bathroom to pull myself together. The horror of what had just happened struck me. I felt dirty—and devastated that he had forced himself on me. When he drove me home that night, he said, "You know you wanted this to happen."

I felt sick and insulted. The next day Carl apologized and said it would never happen again, but he had realized that all he had to do to get sex was first get me wasted, and then he could have his way with me. And that's what happened. After the second time, I resigned myself to the thought that I would just have to marry him. To seal the deal, Carl gave me a gorgeous diamond ring that looked like an engagement ring. It was only a promise ring, but it made me feel special—and in my mind it justified our intimate relationship. Carl's parents loved me, and I could see us one day marrying and being one big happy family.

I had been afraid of becoming pregnant from the minute Carl first started pressuring me to have sex, and it wasn't long before I had a pregnancy scare. Carl knew exactly what to do: he took me to a clinic to get birth control. He was taking good care of me. At least that's what I thought.

Though Carl wasn't my ideal, being with him definitely had its perks. He came from a wealthy family, drove an expensive sports car, lived in an upscale neighborhood, and often showered me with gifts. I was living the lifestyle of the rich and popular girls I had admired for months. Becoming Carl's wife, I would be driving a nice car and belong to the country club, a life I had only dreamed about living. I truly believed that being rich—and having no money problems at all—would bring me true happiness. On my birthday Carl got me a diamond necklace, and soon thereafter he gave me diamond earrings to match. I figured if I married him, at least I would be set for life. After all, he would eventually inherit his father's business.

One big problem, however, overshadowed all these perks: Carl had a nasty temper.

The first time he slapped my face, I was shocked. He quickly apologized and acted as if it had never happened. Confused, I didn't know what to think. I accepted his word that it would not happen again. I tried to move on, but it happened again and again, with each incident worse than the time before.

One evening at a party, Carl accused me of flirting with another boy. Grabbing me, he pushed me—hard—into the porch railing, the whole time yelling at me that I had humiliated him in front of everyone. People stared in our direction. Embarrassed, I quickly mumbled that I was sorry. A guy named Mark kept me from being hurt any more seriously when he came over and asked if I was all right. I nodded, feeling grateful to him for caring about what happened to me. I should have broken up with Carl right then and walked off with Mark, my hero, but after Carl calmed down, I once again forgave him.

As time passed, being with Carl became more of a nightmare. One weekend, as he drove my car, he thought I was checking out the guy driving beside us. He grabbed my hair and pushed my head into the dashboard. I screamed. I desperately wanted to get out of the car, but he wouldn't stop driving. Instead, he actually tried to push me out the door while the car was still moving. I was terrified. Finally, he stopped the vehicle. We argued until both of us said we were sorry.

The most humiliating evening was when I was with a girlfriend at a nightclub. I started talking to a couple of guys who were sitting nearby. All of a sudden someone grabbed me by my hair and dragged me out the door. It was Carl, and he was furious. His eyes, dark with anger, scared me. He pushed me into the street and, swearing at me, called me every vulgar name he could think of. A large crowd of people stared. It was awful. I felt like a piece of trash. My girlfriend rescued me: she rushed over, pulled me out of the street, and helped me to her car while I sobbed. As she drove me home, she encouraged me to break up with Carl. I heard and I understood what she was saying, but I didn't know if I had the courage or the strength to do it.

Later that night, Carl showed up at my house, said he was sorry, and once again told me that he would never do that again. I felt sick to my stomach and hopeless. I seemed stuck in a maze that I couldn't find my way out of. Without realizing it, I had become one of the 1.8 million women in the United States who are abused every year. Foolishly, I continued to date Carl. It's not easy to explain why, and now that I am out of that dysfunctional cycle, it's even more difficult for me to understand what I was thinking. But at the time I felt so beaten down that I thought there would never be anyone else who could love me. So I tried hard to make myself believe that Carl would eventually become a stable, charming boyfriend, but the truth was... I was stuck.

After graduating from high school, I attended a nearby junior college in order to be close to Carl. I also began working as an aerobics instructor at a health club where I made new friends with some of my coworkers. As much as I tried to hide the abusiveness of my relationship with Carl, my older and wiser coworkers soon realized what was going on. One of the health club members—a policeman—mentioned that he had received several domestic disturbance calls regarding Carl's older brother who was having some major fights with his new wife. I also learned that Carl's father often hit Carl's mother. Clearly, there was a family pattern of abuse.

"If he hits you before you're married, he's going to hit you even more after you're married," one friend told me. "It only gets worse."

After all I had suffered from Carl's hand, any attraction I'd ever had toward him had evaporated. Finally I realized that his wealthy lifestyle, his gifts, and the short spurts of positive attention he gave me just weren't worth the pain, the agony, the fear. For all I knew, one day I might lose my life at the hands of this violent man. Though in many ways I was used to his volatile temper, the thought of actually living with such an unstable person for the rest of my life overwhelmed me. I wanted out, but I was afraid. And I simply didn't know how to end our relationship.

About this time I met James, a twenty-eight-year-old client at the health club. He seemed to be a true gentleman, and whenever he was near, I felt safe. It seemed that he would protect me if things got out of hand with Carl. Furthermore, the possibility of dating James gave me the courage to tell Carl I no longer wanted to see him. Thanks to daily aerobics classes, my body was in the best shape it had ever been, and I was feeling confident. Confident enough to believe I could do better than a boyfriend who beat me up. In fact, I was hoping James would be part of that "better." Rumors were, he had a crush on me and would ask me out on a date if I didn't have a boyfriend. I made myself available to talk whenever James was at the gym, and the more I got to know him, the more I wanted to date him. This hope of having a future with James was the incentive I needed to finally break up with Carl.

So, encouraged by my friends as well, I handed Carl back the promise ring a few days later when we were at my parents' house. I told him it was over between us, that I'd had enough. For a moment he just stared at me. Then his eyes darkened and narrowed into a hateful expression. He reached over and yanked at the diamond necklace I wore, a gift from him. I quickly took it off and set it in the palm of his hand, feeling relieved. It was as if giving back the necklace symbolized the end of our relationship. Carl stormed out the door and sped off, leaving tire marks in the driveway. I breathed a huge sigh of relief and enjoyed a sense of freedom that I hadn't felt for a long time. *That hadn't gone as badly as I expected*, I thought to myself.

The next day, though, I remembered that Carl had some inappropriate and highly embarrassing photos of me. I needed to get them back as soon as I could. I called Carl telling him I would stop by his house to pick up some of my things, and I emphasized that I wanted all of the photos back. He agreed to meet with me. To be on the safe side, I took a girlfriend with me.

I walked up to the front door of his parents' home. Carl answered my knock. He had sunglasses on, but he had obviously been crying. He handed me a box of my things, including the photos. I vowed at that very moment that I would never ever pose naked for pictures, no matter how much I thought I loved a guy and no matter how long I had been dating him. I never wanted to be in this position ever again! Thankfully, Carl had willingly handed the photos over for me to destroy. I do feel for those girls who do not get their inappropriate photos or videos back….

As I turned to go back to my car, Carl's mother came out and grabbed my arm, digging her fingernails into my flesh. She told me what she thought of me, and her remarks weren't too flattering. That horrible feeling of being utterly defeated came over me again. Quickly my girlfriend came to my rescue: she jumped out of her car and asked if there was a problem. As Carl's mother loosened her grip, I pulled away and ran to the car.

Later that day, his mother called my mom to tell her how foolish I was to dump Carl. She reminded my mom that I would not only lose out on the family fortune, but that I would absolutely never find anyone as fine as her son. My mother was surprised by the conversation—she had no idea what I had gone through with this guy—and pleased that I was no longer dating this boy. I had wasted three years of my life. Thankfully, he wasn't going to get one more day of it.

The incredible freedom I felt when I finally broke off the relationship told me that I had definitely done the right thing. As the days passed, I began to relax and smile more. I also realized that I had a new lease on life. Good friends and the blossoming of my relationship with James encouraged me to believe that I wouldn't end up alone and unhappy. Hoping he would be the man to rescue me from all my problems, I found myself believing that if James were my soul mate, my life would be complete.

Chapter 3

Getting Even

On my first date with James, he took me on a day cruise to the Bahamas. Dinner, drinks by the pool, and sightseeing on the island made me feel like royalty. Ten years older than me, this dark, handsome, muscular man made me feel safe and secure. I was thrilled that this wealthy and established hunk of a man was interested in me! Unlike Carl, James was drop-dead gorgeous! I had to pinch myself to see if I were dreaming. *Could this man really be interested in me?* I could definitely see myself falling in love and marrying this guy.

It wasn't long, however, before I started hearing rumors that James was involved in drug trafficking. I simply didn't believe it, and I saw absolutely nothing that would back up the rumors. During our dates he drank a little, but never once did I see him use or sell drugs. I hoped this was only vicious gossip—but there was one behavior, one red flag, that I totally ignored. James would abruptly leave town for business, and he would never explain what he was doing or where he was going. Still, I didn't really care what people were saying about James. I thought he was fantastic; I loved and adored him. *James involved in a drug trafficking ring?* No, I just couldn't see it. Or maybe I didn't want to.

During a wonderful month of dating James, I floated along on a cloud of happiness. Then, totally unexpectedly—there hadn't been any sign of trouble—James suddenly stopped calling. I was devastated. I spent hours reviewing in my mind our last time together, wondering what I had done. *Maybe it was that I was only eighteen and still living at home with my parents.* I thought for sure this could be the problem. When I consulted with friends, they were just as shocked about James distancing himself as I was—and they agreed with my theory.

So, motivated to get James back, I moved into a studio apartment with a coworker, hoping to prove I was an adult and draw James back to me. Besides, I needed to escape my parents' disapproving eyes. Now I would be free to make my own decisions and live my life as I wanted to. And I hoped that the next time I saw James at the club to work out, he'd get wind of my newfound freedom. When he did finally show up, I made my presence known when he was on the bench press. Our eyes met and we both smiled, but that was it.

A week later at a Halloween party, I dressed in a sexy pirate costume. James was there, and I hoped to grab his attention. But instead James's best friend Tony started flirting with me. I noticed James glancing our way, looking uncomfortable and even a bit jealous. That was exactly what I'd hoped for! I acted as though I didn't notice his glares, excited to finally get his attention!

My heart skipped a beat as this strong, handsome man walked toward me. When he told me how nice I looked, I said, "Well, thank you" with an attitude suggesting that I didn't really care that he was talking to me—but actually I wanted to jump into his arms. I kept my composure as James offered to get me a drink. As soon as he walked away, Tony reappeared and started telling me jokes. Flattered that two guys were vying for my attention, I thought I might just win James back if this continued—and it did. Later in the evening, though, it escalated into a huge confrontation. When Tony backed off, I had James's full attention. When the party ended, James invited me to his place. I readily accepted, becoming intimate with him for the first time. *Yes! Mission accomplished!* My plan had worked: I had James back in my life once again.

In the morning as he drove me back to my apartment, he seemed unusually quiet. I assumed he was feeling hung over, but as he dropped me off at my apartment, he explained he had a date that evening with a friend of mine, a girl he really liked. He rambled on about how drunk he had been the previous night and that our time together had been a mistake.

⟵⟶

My jaw dropped. *What? I can't be hearing this!* Embarrassed and humiliated, I wanted to melt into the car's seat and disappear. I had naively believed that James and I were getting back together. Instead, he was dumping me. I had only been a one-night stand…. And I had learned not only how horrible that felt but also what cruelty men are capable of. In just a matter of hours, they can love a girl and leave her. *Wow, stupid me. I thought James cared.*…I felt used and utterly alone. I didn't cry, but inside me a tiny seed of bitterness took root. From that point on, I looked at men differently.

Sitting alone in my apartment, depressed and hung over, I thought about how James had used me for his own pleasure… for a brief encounter… and then discarded me. And I wondered how I was going to survive without a boyfriend. I hadn't been single for three years. I hurt deep down to my core, and I wanted to hurt him back. I wanted to get even: I wanted James to pay for the way he had treated me….

When his friend Tony, a bartender at a club I frequently went to with friends, asked me out, I decided to go even though I wasn't particularly attracted to him—and I did hope our dating would bother James. My friends encouraged me to pursue the relationship with Tony. They thought he was very attractive and that I was lucky to be dating him. But, to me, Tony was nothing special. He was only a bartender who didn't make anywhere near as much as money as James did. Still, this could be the perfect way to get even with James. *I'm going to rub this in his face for sure.*

To my surprise, after I'd had a few drinks, Tony started looking pretty good to me, and as I got to know him better, I actually found his blue eyes very appealing. A total romantic, he made our times together special. Often he stopped by to watch me teach aerobics at the health club where I worked. Whenever I saw his smiling face at the window, a warm feeling came over me. I began wanting to see him more and more. Never had I felt this way. Before I knew it—after only a few weeks of knowing Tony, after only a handful of dates—I was completely under his spell.

One day, however, my eyes were opened to the real Tony. A huge red flag popped up right in front of me, but I didn't heed the warning that Tony was not the man for me. The warning had come too late: I was already overcome by his charm....

One morning after school, I was driving a classmate home. She happened to live in the same apartment complex as Tony's ex-girlfriend—his live-in girlfriend for the past three years. Recently Tony and she had broken up. At least that's what he'd told me.

When I drove into the parking lot, I thought I saw Tony's car. Puzzled, I walked over and peeked into the window. Yes, it was definitely his car, but he was supposed to be sleeping at his apartment and meeting me in an hour.... Determined to get to the bottom of this, I drove to his apartment earlier than expected. I wanted to know the truth. I sat outside the door of his apartment and waited. Sure enough, a few minutes later Tony walked up wearing his work uniform from the previous night. I knew immediately that he had not come home after his evening shift but had instead gone to his former girlfriend's apartment.

I confronted him. Sheepishly, he admitted to having spent the night with his ex, but he swore he'd slept on the couch. Tony explained that he still loved her but was not "in love" with her anymore. He convinced me they were simply good friends and that he was only there because she needed to talk. His blue eyes pleaded with me to understand, and I so wanted to believe him that—against my better judgment—I decided to trust him. Tony hugged me and whispered in my ear, "Will you be my only girlfriend?"

My heart did a little flip-flop, and I nodded, tears in my eyes.

For three months Tony and I spent as much time together as possible. I enjoyed the closeness. Spending almost every night at his apartment, I felt as if we were a married couple. On our dates he seemed proud of the fact that I was his girlfriend, and I was proud to have him as my boyfriend. We dined at four-star restaurants, drank champagne, and danced at the fanciest nightclubs. We made a very attractive couple that people noticed. To my surprise, he made more money bartending than I thought, and he had no problem spending it on me. I was enjoying this relationship, and I hoped it would only get better.

One evening Tony was going to visit his mother for her birthday. I thought it was sweet, his wanting to spend time with his mom. But when my girlfriend asked me why he hadn't invited me along, I became suspicious. She'd made a good point. After all, we'd been dating for quite a while.

Well, after several drinks at the bar with my girlfriend, I mustered up enough curiosity to drive by Tony's apartment. I stumbled to my vehicle, once again on a mission to know the truth about Tony. When I pulled into the parking lot, I saw his ex-girlfriend's car parked beside his. I couldn't believe it! It couldn't be her car—but it was. I parked the car, climbed out, and marched to his door. Anger burned in my chest as I pounded on the doorbell over and over again. No one answered. Furious, I threw my car keys at his bedroom window so hard that the glass cracked. Oops, I had gotten a little carried away with my temper, but I was a bit tipsy....

Tony glared out the window. I could see him standing there with a sheet wrapped around his waist and a stunned expression on his face. "Surprise! It's your loving and trusting girlfriend!" I screamed. Hurt and angry, I felt my temper rise to a dangerous level. I definitely could have hurt him! I had trusted Tony; I had believed that he truly loved me. He'd even bought me a ring, saying he wanted to have an exclusive relationship with me. *What kind of human being is this?* I thought.

When Tony walked outside to talk to me, I ran up to him, punched his chest several times, and screamed, "You liar!" I took off toward the parking lot to find my car. He followed me, rambling words, trying to make me feel better, but at that point I knew that everything he said was a lie. Soon his ex-girlfriend came running up, saying, "Come on, Tony. It's my night to be with you."

Stunned and disillusioned, I climbed into my car and slammed the door. I yelled at the top of my lungs, "You liar! I trusted you! We are done!" Tony tried to explain, but I started the engine and sped away. Tears poured down my face, making it difficult for me to drive. My heart was pounding even though it seemed to have sunk into my stomach. I felt nauseous and exhausted. Somehow I reached my driveway safely.

Then, as I lay in bed and thought about the whole situation, the more unbelievable it seemed that his ex-girlfriend had actually agreed to share him with me. I felt sick inside. My innocent trust had been rudely stripped away. Never would I have imagined Tony treating me this way....

The next morning Tony arrived at my door with a beautiful gold necklace and flowers. Proclaiming that he had broken off his relationship with his ex for good, he begged me to give him another chance. Hurting as deeply as I was, his words were a healing balm to my aching heart, and I foolishly decided to give him another chance. After all, I loved him, and I hoped to marry him one day.

But only a week later, when Tony was supposedly playing basketball with his buddies, I received a phone call from his ex telling me that she and Tony were still seeing each other. I could hear Tony in the background screaming at her to hang up. I was in utter shock: I had fallen in love with a compulsive liar. He stormed out of her apartment as she and I continued to talk. For hours—and I was totally stunned the whole time—I listened to her talk about their relationship. The man I thought I knew was leading a double life. When he wasn't with me, he was spending time with her. Soon my phone beeped: someone was calling in. It was Tony, trying to interrupt our conversation. I'd had enough of him, and I told him to leave me alone. His little threesome was over!

Emotionally wounded, I was grateful to have a distraction: I needed to focus all my energy and time on preparing for a national aerobics contest in Miami. I had made it to the finals, one of the top seven out of seventy-five contestants. I was proud of this accomplishment, and the competition was exactly what I needed to get over Tony.

When I was on stage, though, I glanced out into the audience, and there sat Tony with friends of ours. Unhappy to see him, I tried hard to avoid him, but after the competition, a group of us went out to dinner to celebrate my victory. Unfortunately Tony came along and made every effort to talk to me. He finally cornered me and told me how proud of me he was. Then, placing a key to his apartment in my hand, he whispered in my ear, "Move in with me." He pleaded and said he would prove that things were truly over with his ex. He seemed utterly sincere, and I wanted to believe him. Thinking perhaps he had finally recognized how wrong and hurtful his unfaithfulness was and had really changed, I refused to listen to that inner voice of caution. Instead, I decided to give Tony another chance: *Maybe, just maybe, we could be happy together this time.*

For a while, our live-in situation was great. Tony worked late into the night bartending, and I would sit at his bar, enjoying a few drinks. Living the partying nightclub lifestyle was tiring, but Tony eventually introduced me to cocaine. After a few lines of fine white powder, I had all the energy I needed for this new and exciting lifestyle. In time, my weight dropped, which I thought was a good perk, but my grades at school also took a nosedive. Eventually I dropped out of college. I was barely handling my work schedule at the health club, and my late nights did not mix well with my morning classes.

Completely obsessed with Tony, night after night I would drink at his bar. In the late hours, I'd do lines of coke to stay awake. As the evening wore on, I would get so wired I couldn't carry on a conversation without stuttering. My hands would shake so badly it became difficult to light a cigarette. At that point I would realize I needed to head home and get some sleep. But as I lay in bed, with my heart pounding out of my chest, my mind raced: I thought of everything and anything! To calm my nerves, I'd smoke a joint. And, yes, I knew all too well that my body was struggling. At the most intense moments, I worried that if I fell asleep, I wouldn't wake up again. The thought of dying terrified me, and I'd find myself praying, "Please, God, help me to sleep and not to die! I'll never do this much partying again!" But after I made it through that night, I would do it all over again the next evening.

You see, I was in love with two things: a man I hoped to marry and the cocaine he gave me. In reality—and I was unaware of it at the time—I was on a slippery slope, sliding out of control into a world of darkness. And to think this wild ride had started with the idea that I'd get even with a man who'd hurt me. I was in the process of losing big-time.

Chapter 4

My Twisted Love Affair

As you've read about my on-and-off relationship with Tony, you've probably wondered if it will ever end. I promise you: this roller coaster did come to a stop, so you don't need to keep screaming to me, "Get off that ride!" I wasn't quite ready...

You have to realize that, to me, my life seemed pretty good. My job at the health club—an elite fitness club, one of the nicest in the area—was extremely satisfying. Members included pro athletes, models, the rich, and the famous. Occasionally the club had me participate in local aerobics contests and even do some modeling for its ads. My aerobics classes were packed full with faithful followers, and many of my clients looked to me for fitness advice in hopes of achieving my tone-tiny figure. No one at work realized that my judgment was clouded from both intimacy with Tony and my dependency on the precious white powder; no one at work had any idea that I was in a twisted love affair with both.

Tony and I had been living together for six months, and I had tried to please him in every way possible. But there was no pleasing him. Even when I shrank down to a size two, he complained that I looked too much like a little girl and not enough like a woman. Still, I believed that if I did everything I could to look my best; Tony would keep his eyes on me and only me. Yet I fell far short of his expectations, and he made rude comments about my acne, saying he would not marry anyone who had any kind of skin blemishes. So I wore makeup, even to bed, and purchased expensive beauty treatments. Every day I worked out for two hours, trying desperately to look my best. I kept my brunette roots bleached, and I regularly visited the tanning salon. I thought I looked pretty good, but I didn't look good enough for Tony.

His rudeness increased. For Christmas I saved up as much money as I could to buy him an expensive gold necklace, one of the most costly gifts I'd ever purchased. He glanced at it, with a dissatisfied—if not disgusted—expression on his face. Looking up at me, he said, "I wish you'd told me you were getting this. I could have chipped in and gotten a nicer one."

I sat there, my heart aching and my fear growing. No matter what I did, it wasn't enough. I could tell I was losing him. The thought of not having Tony in my life seemed unbearable, but the more I tried to please him, the more he criticized me. Not only was I losing him, but in the process I also was losing my own feeling of self-worth and dignity. Sadder than that loss was the fact that I didn't even realize it was happening.

———

The day came when Tony told me we needed to take a break. He wanted me out of his apartment, and he wanted his key back. Crushed, but clinging to the hope that we could work through this, I agreed and gave him back the key to his apartment. With no place to go, I moved back into my parents' house. Stifling my tears, I pretended to be happy about the fact that I was home again.

It wasn't soon before I learned that Tony was dating someone else. Seeing how down I was, my friend Kate encouraged me to go out on the town with her and some friends. I hadn't spent much time with Kate since she'd started dating my ex-boyfriend James. Kate and James seemed happy together, which was hard for me to watch. I wished I were in a happy, stable relationship like they were. Needing to get Tony off my mind, though, I reluctantly agreed. I went to a club with James, Kate, and a few of their friends.

After several drinks, we made the impulsive decision to go to the Bahamas to gamble. There were eight of us: James, Kate, her sister June, June's boyfriend, and three of James's male friends. Around midnight, without bothering to pack, we climbed aboard a boat and left. An uneasy feeling came over me as the city lights faded and we headed into a wall of eerie darkness. Only a few stars were lighting the way for us. June's boyfriend, stumbling about as he steered the boat, kept teasing us, saying we had run out of gas. We girls would scream, pretending we were afraid that we'd been stranded in the middle of the ocean. Never before had I done anything this foolish! I had unwisely put my life into the hands of this drunk! I wanted to ask him to turn the boat around and take me back to land, but I kept quiet. I swallowed my fears and grabbed another beer, hoping to drink away my anxiety.

James encouraged me to talk to one of his friends who was on the boat, a pleasant man who was married. No way was I going to be a part of that! I knew all too well how it felt to be cheated on, and I was not going to do that to his wife. Unfortunately, this married man was drunk and hanging all over me. In spite of his efforts, I firmly let him know I was off limits. The positive attention I received from all the guys, though, did help salve my damaged ego, but at the same time, I figured each of them was just being nice in order to try to get me into his bed. The seed of bitterness that had been planted in me when I broke up with James had sprouted and grown considerably since my recent breakup with Tony. My body language made it obvious that I was not going to be sleeping with anyone that night. I was perfectly clear about that.

When we finally reached the island marina, a man with a machine gun slung over his shoulder guided our boat to the dock. I was alarmed until James hollered out the man's name. The fact that James seemed to know him eased my concern. We climbed out of the boat and looked around. The marina was like a ghost town; all the windows and doors of every building were boarded up. I kept quiet. I didn't ask any questions, but I knew something was not right. Those inner cautions, though, are easily tossed to the wind when you're under the influence of drugs and alcohol. I had a chemically-induced *"Oh well! I'm young and having fun"* attitude.

Out front a taxi waited to take us to a casino. We piled in and headed off. It never crossed my mind that I was in the Bahamas without showing anyone my passport. *Oh well! I'm having fun!* After hours of gambling, we were drunk and exhausted. James, Kate, and I—along with James's married friend—got a hotel room for the night. My goal to forget about Tony wasn't working very well. In truth, I couldn't stop thinking about him. I kept to myself, drifting into an uneasy sleep, wishing that Tony were with me.

Early the next morning—and not giving us any details—James and his buddies left to do some business. Remembering the rumors I had heard about James's involvement in drug trafficking, I wondered what kind of business they were taking care of. And remembering the way they flashed money around at the casino last night, I knew intuitively that those rumors could be true. *Oh well! It's too late to worry about it now,* I thought, once again choosing a relaxed, carefree attitude.

Kate found a note from James that he had left on the dresser: "Girls, take the cash and go shopping for whatever you need. Meet you for lunch by the pool." Momentarily forgetting about my heartache, I was thrilled to have the opportunity to go shopping. Kate and I grabbed the cash and headed for the shopping district to buy swimsuits, sunglasses, and hats. I felt like a celebrity as I lay out by the pool with my designer swimsuit on, soaking up the sun, enjoying the rock waterfall in the middle of the pool and the bright blue ocean shimmering in the distance. *What would Tony think if he could see me now? Maybe I could do better than him,* I thought. Yet, in spite of everything, I missed him.

At lunch we met up with the guys and headed to a small island to swim in the crystal clear ocean and drink tequila. The sapphire blue sky was beautiful. It was a glorious day. We all drank too much, but somehow made it back to the Florida coast that evening. Thinking back, I am thankful for God's protection. I know He watched over me during that risky adventure.

A jealous Tony called me the next day to ask if I would meet him for lunch. I readily agreed. James had told him all about our adventure in the Bahamas. I could tell he was relieved to hear I had been faithful to him during the trip because at lunch he insisted that I move back to his place. *He really had missed me,* I thought to myself. I never asked him about the new girl. Figuring that his relationship with her hadn't worked out, I naively told myself that he had finally realized that he truly loved me—and only me. That afternoon I packed my bags and settled back in where I believed I belonged.

———

The best predictor of a person's future behavior is that person's past behavior. Maybe you've heard those wise words before. Well, I didn't heed them. I preferred to keep my head in the sand. I didn't want to believe the worst. I guess I hadn't yet had enough of this twisted love affair....

A few months later Tony suddenly decided to work in Long Island, New York, for the summer. He had family there, and he'd visit friends. He asked me to go, but he knew I wouldn't want to give up my job at the health club. So I stayed behind to work and take care of his apartment.

The summer seemed to drag along. I was desperately missing Tony, and that pain was especially sharp when I attended two weddings. My friends had found their soul mates. I was envious. I so longed to be engaged to Tony. Dealing with the ache of my loneliness, I did a lot of partying with friends, but I never hooked up with anyone. Even though I had opportunities, I refused to cheat on Tony. And Tony was calling me regularly. I missed him dearly. He said he missed me too.

I was excited when I made arrangements to meet him in New York. Dressed to impress, I hoped he would like what he saw when I stepped off the plane. The minute I saw him, I ran and jumped into his arms. It felt wonderful. We drove to the place he had rented, a small room, only a third the size of his apartment back home—and he had to share the bathroom with all the other tenants. Though there was a tiny ocean view from his bedroom window, I was surprised that he liked living in such cramped quarters, but I kept my thoughts to myself. I was determined to just enjoy his company.

But it didn't take me long to realize that Tony wasn't happy having me there. Everything I did annoyed him, so I spent most of my time alone. I'd go to the beach or sit at the club where he worked, not talking to anyone.

He hated it when I talked with other men while he worked. It kept him from concentrating on what he was doing. Then, when we were alone, his emotions were erratic. One minute he would yell at me. Then he'd avoid me. It was as if I didn't even exist. And in the next moment he'd ask me to slow dance and be very romantic. I couldn't figure out what was wrong with him.

On my last night in New York, I dreamed that I found a picture of him with a girl. Written on the back of the photo was "Love, Alisha." The next morning I told him about the dream and described what the girl had looked like. He paled and became very distant. All the way to the airport, he barely spoke. Something was definitely wrong between us. During the flight home, I had a sick feeling in my gut: I knew that Tony was involved with someone else. I was tired of being treated this way. One day he loved me; the next day he hated me....

I arrived home with a bad headache—and the long, hard cry I had didn't help. Lying in the bed I had once shared with Tony, with a severe migraine headache raging, I wanted to curl up in a ball and die. I didn't want to talk to anyone—ever. I couldn't bear to tell my friends what I suspected. Besides, I was convinced they were tired of hearing my woes about this twisted relationship. And I realized they were right: Tony was no good for me—but I was afraid to let go. What else did I have?

That evening I had another dream that seemed so real I wasn't sure whether I had dreamed it or actually lived it. In my dream, I climbed out of bed, walked to the sliding glass door, and pulled back the blinds. In the sky was a beautiful bright light, and angels were flying toward me. Warmth, peace, and love fell over me in a blanket of comfort. When I woke the next morning, I knew I needed to move out of Tony's apartment. This relationship had to end.

———◦———

With my heart breaking, I packed my things and headed back to live with my parents. The next three months were a blur. I didn't talk to Tony or return his phone calls. I worked, partied with friends, and numbed my pain. Eventually, though, I broke down and answered one of his calls. Tony was coming home from New York, and he wanted me to meet him at his apartment. I bit my lip, unsure. But, lonely and vulnerable, I finally agreed to see him.

When Tony walked through the door and hugged me, acting as if he had really missed me, I felt in my heart as if I were home again. I melted into his arms, enjoying the strong physical connection we had always enjoyed. Afterward, as we sat on the bed to talk, he told me he wanted to be honest. I smiled, feeling myself relax, convinced he was about to tell me how much he loved me and that he wanted me back for good.

"That dream you had in New York really freaked me out," he said. "I've been seeing a girl. Her name is Alisha. She looks just like the girl you described to me from your dream."

My heart sank. This was not what I wanted to hear.

"I'm moving back to New York," he continued. "Alisha and I are planning to live together."

My stomach turned inside out.

"She'll be calling me in a few minutes, so it would be best if you went ahead and left now. It wouldn't be right for you to be here while we talk."

I stared at him in utter shock. *It wouldn't be right? What would she think about what he and I had done only fifteen minutes earlier?* My heart splintered into a million pieces. Too stunned to say anything, I slowly gathered my things and went back to my parents' house.

The next day when Tony called—I'm ashamed to say—I went back to see him. I desperately wanted to win him back. He said he loved me but that he needed to find himself. My self-respect already gone, I gave myself physically to him once again, but it did no good. I felt used and stupid when he told me that the Alisha would be flying down to help him move. *What was wrong with me? I continually came back for more of his abuse? Why do I let him keep treating me like trash?* Enraged—at him, at myself—I pounded on his chest and cursed him with every nasty word I could think of. I stormed out of his apartment and headed to the nearest bar for a drink.

After Tony moved to New York, I was overwhelmed by depression. Wanting to feel better, I began drinking heavily. One night after a party I embarrassed myself in the parking lot by yelling at the bouncer, "My car's been stolen. I parked it right here, and now it's gone." The bouncer insisted he had been there all evening and no Volkswagens had ever come into the lot. I stood there, trying to clear my head, wondering where my car could be when it hit me; it had to be at the party down the road. Not thinking about my safety, I started running. Several people stared, but I just kept running. About three miles down the road, I reached the club and found my car. I climbed behind the wheel and drove to my parents' house. I don't know how I made it home that night, but I did.

The next day, Tony called me, saying that he was returning my phone call. I was so hung over, and my head was pounding. *I had called him? When?* He said I had left a long message on his answering machine. I cringed. I had absolutely no memory of calling him. I must have blacked out. I talked to a girlfriend who had been with me and asked her to help me to remember what had happened. She simply told me that I had acted like a drunken fool.

"You have a drinking problem, Chrissie," she insisted.

I ignored her. I didn't have a drinking problem. I could control myself if I wanted to.

The truth is, it was on those nights when cocaine was available that I couldn't control myself. Snorting cocaine made me feel like I was on top of the world. Those nights when, high on cocaine, I stayed up all night dancing my woes away were my favorites. Cocaine wasn't cheap, so whenever it was offered to me, I had a hard time saying no. And why would I ever turn down something that I loved so much? One afternoon a friend even caught me digging through the trash for straws that had been used to snort cocaine the previous evening. When I found one, I cut it open and licked the residue of white powder.

"You're sick, Chrissie," she said.

I laughed, not taking her words seriously. I just wanted to numb my pain. I suppose my drug use was a form of self-medicating, but I ignored the obvious: I was becoming a drug addict.

During this time I allowed myself to have several one-night stands. Perhaps that was another form of self-medicating, but they always left me feeling empty and alone. I kept hoping Tony would come back to me. And one day he surprised me by visiting me after he'd had an argument with his girlfriend, a big argument that had sent him back to Florida for a visit. But a really odd thing happened. The moment I saw Tony, I just stood there, staring at him. I realized that, for the first time ever, I felt absolutely no attraction toward him. Something in me had changed. He talked about moving back to Florida, but I realized I didn't care. At last… finally… I didn't care about that man.

The stronghold he once had on me had been broken. I realized that I no longer loved Tony. I didn't want him or need him back in my life. I wanted someone better—someone who would treat me better. *There has to be someone out there for me, someone who would sweep me off my feet, who would love and adore me, who would be faithful and loyal.* Well, at least I *hoped* there was a guy like that out there.

Chapter 5

The Getaway

We lived in two separate worlds that were radically different from each other. I was used to a fast-paced, club-hopping, drinking and partying, doing-what-I-wanted-to-do-when-I-wanted-to-do-it lifestyle. Of course I found living with my parents and their sedate, Lutheran ways unbearable. To say we often clashed is a huge understatement. Our relationship had long been one where they preached at me, treating me like the child I once had been. I despised listening to their lectures on how I should live or how I needed Jesus. Their words of supposed wisdom had nothing to do with what I was going through. I didn't want their advice, nor did I think it would help me. I believed that my parents were just out to ruin my life, so I avoided them as much as possible.

My parents were unaware of my drug use—I'm not sure they even knew what cocaine was—but they knew that I drank. They often saw me hung over and hugging the toilet. Being of legal drinking age, I didn't feel the need to hide the evidence of my nighttime activities, and they didn't say much to me about it—which was a good thing. I probably would have snapped their heads off! For the most part, we kept our distance from one another and barely spoke.

I knew I had disappointed them with the choices I had made—and was continuing to make—but I tried not to let it bother me. I told myself it wasn't my fault, that I was only trying to survive in this crazy world. Not wanting to ask them for money, I worked hard as a waitress during the day and as an aerobics instructor in the evenings. Usually I let them know where I was going, and I checked in from time to time so they wouldn't bother waiting up for me. Looking back, I can see how they were actually sick with worry. My father got up for work at four o'clock most mornings, and that was often the time I was getting home after a night of partying. I'd try to sneak into the house and shower away the stale smoke smell before I hit the bed, and all the while I was hoping he wouldn't notice how late I'd been out. I hated the way he—and my mom—would look at me with those disapproving but concerned eyes.

———

My parents irritated me. They hounded me to go to church, acting as if doing so would help me have a happier life! As far as I could tell, religion hadn't done much for them! There they were, lower middle class, blue-collar workers in one of the richest cities in the United States. I, however, much preferred hanging with the upper class and enjoying the perks that the rich enjoyed. So I brushed off their suggestions, convinced that I would be just fine without religious nonsense. Living under their roof, I bottled up my frustrations and hostility, yet those emotions festered inside me and often boiled over when I was in the same room with them. My parents couldn't possibly understand me! Obviously we wanted very, very different things out of life!

Each Friday evening, for instance, several couples—friends of my parents—came over for Bible study. They sat in the living room as I got ready to go out to the clubs. Sometimes I would loudly yell cuss words just to shock them. Then, wearing what they would undoubtedly consider a horrendously immodest outfit, I'd strut through the living room on my way out to the jungle of the nightclub scene, where I always hoped to catch a buzz and meet a rich guy. These dear folks all sat, watching and—I'm sure now—saying a silent prayer for me. I shook my head as I backed out of the driveway. I thought my parents were old fashioned, living in a little cocoon world, not enjoying life. I laughed to myself. *Bible study—what a waste of their time!*

But, when I was able to be honest with myself, I had noticed that this late-night partying with this same group of friends at the same clubs was actually starting to get a little old—and depressing. I was 22 years old and still single, and nothing in my life held out much promise that I'd ever find my soul mate. *I need a change or I'll go crazy! I need to get away from my parents—and from everything that reminds me of Tony.*

<hr />

One evening a friend called and asked me if I might be interested in teaching aerobics to kids at a camp in the mountains of North Carolina this summer—and I jumped at the opportunity. The next morning I went for an interview and was hired. I was ecstatic! I was finally escaping my parents and all their God talk! After I found a substitute to cover my aerobics classes for the summer, everything was set. I couldn't wait to pack my bags and be gone....

And my destination was amazing. The mountain resort, with trees that towered over me, was beautiful. The campground had a small lake with a waterfall, glistening creeks, and twisting walking trails, reminding me of paths I had walked as a child in Iowa. The weather, neither too hot nor too cold, was just right. I smiled: I was convinced this would be a great getaway.

Assigned to a cabin with three other girls, I felt content. Yes, this would be a new start. As I unpacked my trunk, I found a Bible tucked inside. Pulling it out, I saw a note my mother had written. I felt annoyed and embarrassed. I showed the Bible to the girls and said, "Hey, look. My religious mother sent me a Bible to read this summer. I know all of you will want to read it too." We all laughed, and I threw it back in the trunk, not wanting to have anything more to do with it.

Eight of us, four girls and four guys, were in charge of the kids' activities. Before the kids arrived, we went camping overnight in the mountains in order to plan and bond—and, boy, did we ever bond! This group loved to party! That night we drank shots of rum by the fire while the guys entertained the girls with stories. It had been a long time since I had enjoyed myself so much. It was a great start to my getaway. I knew this would be a summer to remember.

<hr />

Weeks passed, and the eight of us became quite close. We partied hard on our days off, making great memories and sharing lots of laughs. It was as if I had known these seven people my whole life!

On the first day off we had, we were hanging out at a local bar, drinking shots, when one of the guys asked me to dance. William was tall, he had sandy brown hair and green eyes, and he was a great dancer. Because of my dance experience, I kept right up with him, and I had an incredible time! Although William wasn't as muscular as the other men I had been attracted to, he did have a charming English accent. We started out dancing to the fast songs, but as the evening progressed, he pulled me in close to dance more intimately. After a particularly soft song, William tried to go in for a kiss.

Having heard he was involved with one of the camp counselors, I backed away and asked, "What about Julie?"

"Oh, we used to date a long time ago, but we're just friends now," he explained.

Those words sounded all too familiar. Briefly I told him that I had heard that story before and it had ended badly. No way was I getting involved in a threesome again! And no way was I stupid enough to buy into that lie! I put up my guardrails real fast, and we immediately stopped dancing. William was a bit thrown, but he didn't give up.

After that incident on the dance floor, he amped up his pursuit, sending me little notes and flowers during the workweek. On the days off that followed, the more I spent time with William, the more I could feel my walls coming down and my heart softening. Julie had different days off and wasn't not able to be with us, and that made it easier for me to believe that maybe they were just friends. Still cautious, I did notice that when Julie was around, he acted as if he and I were just friends. I understood that he didn't want her to feel uncomfortable, and I was fine with that arrangement. I sure didn't want any girl drama. Besides, I knew exactly how it felt to see your ex hanging all over a new girlfriend, so I was careful not to get affectionate with William in front of Julie or her coworkers. Only the eight of us who had the same days off knew that William and I were more than friends.

By the end of the summer, I was in love. I didn't want our time together at camp to end, and I dreaded the thought of returning to my parents' home. On the last day of camp, William and I exchanged phone numbers, and he promised to call me regularly. I gave him a card to read on his flight home. In it I told him how much our time together meant to me. I dreamed all the way home that I would be the one to officially make him a US citizen. (William's visa had run out, but he had managed to find a good job in Austin, Texas, working with a friend from England.) I hoped he would truly miss me and want me to join him in Texas as his wife one day soon.

⌒

When I got back in Florida, I was tormented by bad memories of Tony. I found myself going through the motions rather than living life. I was physically in Florida, but my head was in Texas as I dreamed of William. We talked on the phone twice a week and planned to see each other over Thanksgiving weekend. I couldn't wait to see him! I was counting the days and getting more and more excited as the day approached. On the plane to Austin, I imagined William asking me to marry him, and while I was visiting, I mentioned that I could relocate to Austin. William clearly told me not to move there on account of him. *What did he mean by that?*

A light bulb went on in my head, flashing its rejection message loud and clear: "He doesn't want me." Once again someone did not feel the same way about me that I felt about him. This time my heart quickly built a wall around itself, hiding my disappointment. I quickly changed the subject, but I definitely understood: I had been just a summer fling, and William hadn't had the guts to tell me. I was thankful when it was time for me to leave. As I boarded the plane, I felt utterly broken.

Why does this keep happening to me? Once again someone had trampled on my heart. I wanted to forget William, but it was hard. Not only did I feel rejected, but now my hopes of getting away from my parents were crushed. I was stuck home with my Jesus-loving mom and dad. Daily I stared at a picture of William and me. We looked like a couple in love. I gazed longingly at that photo and wondered if William had just pretended to love me. If all that was pretend, he should consider acting as a career! He had me thoroughly convinced that he loved me, but I was wrong.

My bitterness grew, and I came to the conclusion that all men are manipulative liars. They would say whatever it took to get a woman into bed. Once again my dreams had been completely shattered. I decided that I would never again trust a man with my heart. I had dated enough of them to know that not one of them—no matter how kindly I treated them, no matter how perfect I made myself, no matter how much I hoped for—could be trusted. I needed to protect myself.

Discouraged with the dating scene and totally disillusioned about men in general, I let my heart harden. I was absolutely ruthless with any male who approached me: I said whatever came to my mind, I didn't care at all about their feelings, and I had no problem saying, "Leave me alone!" I was done joining in their little games of manipulation. No longer was I a toy to be played with! I was sick and tired of being used and abused! So, drink after drink, line after line of cocaine, party after party with friends, I acted as if I were happy, but I was only trying to numb my trampled-on heart.

Chapter 6

The Voice

I was depressed and angry. When I looked at my life, I didn't like what I saw. At twenty-three, I was a college dropout, single, hating men with a vengeance, and feeling lost and lonely. Girls I graduated with from high school were coming home with a college degree, a career, and a fiancé. I had been so focused on partying that I hadn't realized how I was wasting irreplaceable years of my life. I had nothing to show for the past four years; I had absolutely nothing to be proud of. I was slowly sinking into a pit of despair, and I had no idea how I would get myself out....

One evening when I was feeling sorry for myself, I came across a mini-series on television about spirits talking to people through their dreams. I was fascinated with what I was watching, and the program got me thinking about spiritual matters. One particular scene caught my attention: a woman was walking on a beach, holding her arms wide apart, and yelling, "God is within me!" How could she say that? At this point in my life, I pictured God stuck in heaven while I was stuck on earth—and at the time I pretty much thought earth was hell.

So how could God be *within* a human being? I tried to remember a Bible story that talked about God being within a person—yes, I had attended church and heard Bible stories—but I couldn't think of one. Since it had been ages since I had been to church, I was stumped by the idea that God might be within this girl. While I was glued to the television, listening intently to every word, my mother joined me on the couch. She had become curious about my infatuation with the program.

One reason for my fascination was the strange coincidence that, for the past year, I had been having dreams that tended to come true, just as the people in the mini-series had experienced. Occasionally, I would dream about one of my friends, and when I talked with her, I'd find out that my dream was amazingly accurate.

Recently, I had had the most bizarre experience ever after a dream. I had dreamed about a plane crashing into the screen porch of a house. The house caught fire, and the pilot lay motionless, bleeding from his forehead. At work that day, I told my coworkers about my dream and described the images that were still in my head. After I finished, we all stopped in our tracks: we were staring at the television above the bar, listening to the news report of a plane crash. The pictures flashing on the screen were identical to the scenes from my dream that I had just described. We were stunned, frozen in place, as we watched the TV. When a customer noticed, she touched my arm lightly. Speaking softly and looking deep into my eyes, she told me I had a special gift. The woman asked if I had ever felt a presence or seen a light. I shook my head.

"If you ever do, go with it. It's nothing bad. It's good."

I didn't know what to think about her odd remark, but as I watched this mini-series, I began to believe that what she said might be true. *Maybe I did have a special gift.* I was so desperate to feel good about myself that this thought gave me a sense of purpose.

When I told my mom about my fascination with the spiritual world, she was concerned. "God has created a spiritual world, Chrissie," she said, "but there's only one Spirit you want to mess with. That's the Holy Spirit."

I didn't comment. Her God-talk was so annoying! But later that night I started thinking about what she said. As I lay there in my room, I decided to try to read my Bible. (Yes, the same Bible I had pulled out of my trunk at camp and disrespectfully tossed back in.)

"Okay, let's try reading this stuff," I decided, opening the cover and flipping to somewhere in the middle. Maybe it was Psalms. I began reading the words, trying to make sense of what they meant, but I couldn't think clearly. It wasn't so much that the words didn't make sense, but the thoughts in my head were all so jumbled and confused.

"You're wasting your time. How is this going to help you? You can't even understand what you're reading," a voice in my mind taunted.

It was as if an angel was on one shoulder and a demon on the other, and a battle raged in my mind. The angel encouraged me to keep reading, while the devil was taunting me, wanting me to stop. Totally unable to concentrate, I finally gave up, threw the Bible to the floor, turned out the lights, and went to bed.

I tossed and turned, unable to sleep. I kept a nightlight on in my room and left the hall light on so I could see any shadow that might appear under my locked bedroom door. Then I'd know if someone were there. These precautions helped me feel safe, but that night it wasn't working....

I had this eerie sensation that someone stood at the foot of my bed. I sat up and looked around. No one was there—but I could feel it. Someone *was* in my bedroom. Freaked out by the idea that some sort of presence was roaming around my room, I decided it would be best to turn on my bedroom light and open the door in case I needed to run down the hall to my parents' room for help.

When I turned the light on, I saw I was very much alone. *It's all in your head,* I told myself. *There's no one here.* I was sure that the television show and all the talk about spirits had just gotten to me. So, with all the lights on, I forced myself to lie back down, but I could still feel it. That presence. That thing. Whatever it was, I was sure it stood right at the foot of my bed, staring at me. Shutting my eyes, I breathed in slowly, trying to relax. *What had that strange lady at work said to me? Something about going with the presence, that it was nothing bad.* The presence, no matter how much I denied it, continued to hover near me. It stayed close to the foot of my bed. Clearly, it was not going away.

Okay, I thought. *I'm going to believe this is God.* As soon as those words flashed through my mind, something shot into my inner ear, giving it a numb sensation. Then that something—that energy—flew through me, taking over my whole body. I could not speak or shout for help. I froze—and I was totally unable to breathe.

"It's time you believe it's God!" a deep voice thundered.

My insides shook at the power emanating from the voice. Terrified, I had broken into a cold sweat. Abruptly the presence left.

Gasping for air, I jumped from the bed and raced to the bathroom. Hurrying past my parents' bedroom, I wondered if I should wake them and tell them what had happened. *No, they would think I've gone crazy. Besides, this couldn't have actually happened. I must have dreamed it.* I stared at my pale reflection in the mirror. *That was no dream. I definitely heard that voice.*

Finally calming down, I forced myself to go back to my bedroom to try to sleep. Leaving all the lights on, I climbed into bed and cuddled under my covers. I shut my eyes, but instead of seeing darkness, I saw big bold letters reading "**Galatians 3:26.**" I opened my eyes and looked around the room. Everything looked normal. When I closed my eyes again, I could still see the Bible verse. I opened my eyes and glanced down at my Bible on the floor. *Should I pick it up?* No, I was too afraid. I just wanted to go to sleep and pretend all this had never happened! The presence, the voice, the Bible verse—none of this could have been real. I had a dream. I must have had a dream.

Exhausted, I shut my eyes. I was so longing for sleep—and I was choosing to ignore the verse that stared at me. As all the lights still blazed in my bedroom, I eventually dozed off into a troubled sleep.

In the morning my mother asked me why I had slept with my lights on. I looked at her concerned face. *What I'm about to share with her is going to freak her out. She is really going to think I've gone nuts.*

As I told her what had happened, I started crying. I was upset and very confused about what had happened.

Calmly, my mom reached for her Bible to look up **Galatians 3:26 NKJV.** *"For you are all sons of God through faith in Christ Jesus."*

"I don't get it," I said. That sentence didn't make sense to me at all.

Mom shook her head. "Chrissie, God is trying to get your attention. You need to go back to church." Genuinely concerned, she said that she would pray for me.

"I'll think about going," I said.

I was not at all sure I was ready to go back to church. But it was Monday, and I had six days until the next church service. *Plenty of time to consider the possibility….*

Still feeling overwhelmed and uneasy about what had happened—or about what I had dreamed—I struggled to gather my thoughts and figure out what to make of it all. The rest of the day I kept to my usual routine, and I didn't tell any of my friends about the voice I'd heard the previous night. In fact, I tried to forget, but by nightfall, I once again found that I could not sleep. Desperately wanting to sleep, I closed my eyes, and tonight the bold letters read "**Jeremiah 1:11**." The letters persisted. Cautiously, I picked up my Bible and turned to that verse. It read: *Moreover the word of the LORD came to me saying, "Jeremiah, what do you see?" and I said, "I see a branch of an almond tree." Then the LORD said to me, "You have seen well, for I am ready to perform My word" (Jeremiah 1:11-12 NKJV).* As I read those verses, it dawned on me: God was talking to me in the same way He had spoken to the prophet Jeremiah generations earlier. I wasn't seeing almond trees, but I was seeing Bible references. The fact that God was ready to *perform* His *word* made me wonder what else He might do.

For five more nights, God gave me a new verse of Scripture, in bold letters, right when I closed my eyes to fall asleep. I was stunned by the fact that the words were always exactly what I needed to hear. It was as though God were reading my mind. I knew that when I prayed silent prayers, God—and only God—could hear what I was saying, and sure enough, this week He answered my prayers with a Bible passage. I couldn't believe this was happening to me! As that first week unfolded, I began to realize that God knew me better than I knew myself. Even though at times I thought I was going crazy, God continued to show Himself to me, revealing to me that He was communicating with me in much the same way He had talked to those in the Bible.

Through dreams, God had talked to Joseph and Daniel. Through a burning bush, He had talked to Moses. Over and over again in Scripture, I saw how God spoke to His people in order to direct their paths. But that had been a long time ago. I didn't know that anything like this could happen in the twentieth century! And having never heard anyone talk about this kind of stuff, I was a little bit afraid that I was turning into some sort of freak.

By Friday I'd had enough of these nighttime events, and I just wanted life to get back to normal. So I decided to go shopping to get my mind off everything. I found the perfect outfit, but even though it was on sale, the price was too high. Lucky for me, a friend of mine who worked at the store gave me a "five-finger discount." She did her magic at the cash register and handed me the outfit free of charge. Thrilled, I left the mall.

That night when it was time to go to bed, I had no desire to pray. The guilt I felt about stealing the outfit weighed heavily on my mind. I wanted God to leave me alone, but my conscience wouldn't let me sleep. Shutting my eyes, I saw "**Galatians 4:9**" written in bold letters. Trying to ignore it, I told myself that I'd already read a verse in Galatians and I really didn't need to read another one. But the verse continued to flash in my mind's eye not giving me peace. Reluctantly I reached for my Bible and read: *But now after you have known God, or rather are known by God, how is it that you turn again to the weak and beggarly elements, to which you desire again to be in bondage?*

Embarrassed, I realized that God knew about the outfit—and exactly how I had gotten it too. I had thought this gorgeous outfit would make me feel better, but it could have gotten me thrown in jail for stealing. For the past five days, I had been talking with God. I was getting to know Him better, and, clearly, He had been talking to me. Instead of appreciating this relationship, though, I had turned back to material things to bring me happiness. I couldn't escape God. He knew me so well that He had directed me to the exact verse that would help me realize what I had done. He was gently trying to keep me from going backwards and, at the same time, encouraging me to move forward with Him. I lay back in bed, feeling very humbled.

By Sunday I had surrendered to the idea of attending church with my parents. When I walked in, I felt totally out of place. As I found a seat in a pew, I saw that engraved on the stone altar was the verse **Galatians 3:26**. *No way, I can't believe this!* That was the same verse I'd been given the first night I'd heard the voice. I relaxed, sensing I was supposed to be here, and during the service, I had the comforting feeling that God Himself sat beside me.

Although I had visited this church several times, I'd usually had difficulty understanding all the songs and rituals, but this time the words made complete sense. It was as though someone had flipped a switch inside my brain.

The sermon that day just happened—although I have since learned that with God nothing "just happens"—to be about how God communicates with His people. The preacher explained that God speaks to some of us like a bolt of lightning and to others of us, in whispers. I could certainly relate to the bolt of lightning method! Deep down in my heart, I realized that God really did speak to people here on earth and that He had actually chosen to speak to me, too. *Maybe I wasn't going crazy after all.*

At the end of the service, I realized that I'd enjoyed what I'd heard, but as I looked around, I saw only people my parents' age. I wondered how I would ever fit in. But I wasn't yet convinced that becoming a church-going Christian would help me find happiness anyway. *What if God wanted to send me off to some foreign country to spend the rest of my life in misery?* Actually, I was convinced that if I became a Christian, my life would be miserable. After all, the only Christians I had ever met were boring, unattractive people. Throughout my life, I tended to avoid them as much as possible. To become one of them—yuck! I definitely needed to take this thing slowly. I was in absolutely no rush to jump into the Jesus-loving lifestyle. Not yet.

Wanting to play it safe, I carefully planned my strategy. I went to church on Sundays, and I read my Bible and prayed in private. I continued to socialize with friends. I only drank small amounts of alcohol from time to time, and I avoided cocaine. I gave myself a mental pat on the back, thinking I was doing pretty well. I'd spend half my time with God, testing this Christian stuff, and I'd spend the other in the world I was used to.

Then, one day as I was leaving work, I ran into a friend who told me that Joe, one of the guys I'd partied with during my summer at camp, was in town visiting his grandmother. "He's a Jesus freak now," she said.

I was in shock! *A friend of William's, a Jesus freak?* I was curious and excited to hear how this had happened. *Could it be that Joe had had an experience like mine?* I asked her how I could get in touch with him, and she gave me his phone number. I couldn't wait to talk to him. *Finally I might have someone who would understand.*

Hurrying home, I dialed his number as soon as I walked in the door. He seemed excited to hear my voice, and we talked for hours, sharing our stories with each other. He was stunned to hear about my experience with God. It was very different from his, but he never made me feel awkward about it. Finally, I had met someone my age who totally understood what I was going through!

We ended our conversation by making plans to meet the following Sunday night at his church. I was a little nervous about seeing Joe. I didn't want him to think I liked him as more than a friend. At this point in my life, I needed a friend, not a *boy*friend. I hoped he would be willing to be that kind of friend.

On Sunday I drove to Joe's church and met him at the entrance. Greeting me with a hug, he walked me into the large auditorium to find a seat. A band on stage played modern music, nothing like what I had heard in my parents' church. People raised their hands and spoke in words I didn't understand. Several even danced in the aisle. Having never seen anything like this before and feeling very uncomfortable, I sat down.

At the end of the service, we were asked to raise our hand if we wanted to accept Jesus into our heart as Lord and Savior. I kept my hand down. I was not ready to take that step. Besides, I'd never heard of this before. I was freaking out! On top of that, my stomach felt sick. And even as God tugged at my heart, I just couldn't raise my hand. I stood there, frozen, struggling, wrestling with God. Part of me wanted to accept Jesus into my life, but another part of me was very afraid of what that would mean.

After the service, Joe asked if I had ever asked Jesus to be my Lord and Savior.

"I didn't know I had to," I told him. I already had a relationship with God. But as Joe talked, I realized that I had never fully surrendered myself to Christ's lordship; I had never given Him total control over my life.

Joe explained to me, "God can talk to anyone He wants to talk to, but when you receive Jesus as your Lord and Savior, He forgives your sins, and you become a child of God. Through faith, trusting Jesus to come into your life, yielding to His guidance to make you what He has destined you to become."

Joe warned me that the devil was fighting for control of my life at the same time that God was tugging at my heart. He explained that if I didn't dedicate my life to Christ, I would be playing a dangerous game. I couldn't just go to church on Sundays, read my Bible, and pray—and then do whatever I wanted to do the rest of the week. Looking me in the eye, he said, "Chrissie, you need to make a choice. Are you going to do what *you* want, or are you going to let God have total control of your life?"

I knew Joe was right. I had one foot in the world, still hoping I would find happiness there, and I had one foot in the boat with Jesus, wondering if I could find happiness with Him. As I climbed into my car, Joe handed me a booklet explaining everything we had talked about. As I drove home, I felt confused. I didn't know if I was ready to make such a huge commitment. I prayed and asked God to help me understand. Asking Jesus into my heart to be my Lord and Savior—that was all new and foreign to me. I needed time to think about this.

Chapter 7

Divided I Stand

I was the rope in a tug-of-war: I was being pulled in two different directions. I thought I could balance time with God *and* time with my friends. And I still believed that I would one day find a rich, handsome man to marry and make all my dreams come true. I was convinced that I knew exactly what I needed to make me happy. I was intrigued by the idea of committing my life to Christ, but I was not at all certain it was the road for me.

Only a few days after my conversation with Joe, my friend Rachel called to set me up on a blind date with her boss. She described him as cute, charming, well-off, and living in Miami. Brent had admired my picture in Rachel's office and asked her to introduce us. Although I was flattered, I just didn't care for blind dates. But since Rachel and I had been friends for a long time, I agreed—*if* she would come with me. She agreed. So we planned to go boating, have lunch, and attend an evening party with Brent the following weekend. He offered us his guest room overnight since Miami was hours away.

Rachel was convinced that Brent and I would make a perfect couple, and her description made me think she might be right. It had been awhile since I had gone on a date, so I was excited and hoping for the best. *Maybe—just maybe Rachel—had found my Mr. Right.*

On the morning we were to leave, Rachel's daughter came down with a stomach virus. I understood why Rachel needed to stay home, but now I was in an awkward situation. I pleaded with her to call Brent and let him know that we were unable to come. Rachel refused, insisting that Brent would be a perfect gentleman and that I would have a wonderful time. I gave up my protests and decided to trust her judgment. She had worked for the man long enough to know his true character, and, for all I knew, I might be letting a great guy get away because of my own uncertainties.

It wasn't long before I received a call from Brent. Rachel had told him about my reluctance to go alone. As he elaborated on the activities he had planned for my visit, his friendly voice helped ease my mind. It sounded as if he had gone out of his way to show me a nice time. I still had a nagging feeling that I ought to back out of this date, but part of me wanted to be adventurous and go in spite of my concerns.

Sick of questioning myself, I decided I wasn't going to let a little uneasiness stop me. The adventurous part of me won the internal debate, and I drove the two hours to Miami. On the way I pictured what Brent might look like and hoped he would be attractive—and if he wasn't what Rachel had said he was, I planned to make her pay for putting me in this position!

After I spent two hours in the car with just stress, anxiety, and worry about the unknown as my company, my emotions were getting the best of me. *I really hope this is going to be worth my time.*

When I reached his condo, Brent was outside, leaning against a black sports car. Dressed stylishly in white shorts and sky blue shirt, he was actually quite attractive! He had dark, curly hair and an athletic body that made me think "tennis player." Also instantly impressed by the lavish accommodations he lived in, I smiled at him and stepped from my vehicle to introduce myself. He smiled back, tipping his sunglasses down, so I could see his brown eyes. Quite the gentlemen, he opened the door of his car, I climbed in, and we headed to a restaurant.

On the way Brent asked if I planned to use his guest room for the night. I thanked him, but said I thought I'd drive home after the party that evening. He said he was glad I had come down in spite of Rachel's absence and seemed thrilled that I had agreed to be his date for the day.

Arriving at a restaurant near the Intracoastal Waterway, we headed to the bar to wait for Brent's friends to arrive in their boat. My nerves were getting the best of me: I felt very awkward and not very hungry at all. Even though Brent seemed nice, I realized how much I feared rejection. I was worried about what he thought about me and whether I met his expectations. I was so tense: I couldn't just relax and enjoy his company. So I gladly accepted the cocktail he offered, hoping the drink would help calm my nerves.

Eventually Brent's friends—a young married couple—joined us. They glanced at me, clearly checking me out, and I felt even more insecure. These were professional, upper-class people, but me? I was nobody! When they asked what I did for a living, I reluctantly told them I taught aerobics. They smiled politely and quickly changed the subject, making me feel completely second-class. I smiled back at them, hoping we would have something in common to talk about. I tried to listen more to what they were saying and keep the focus on them, not me. That strategy seemed to work: they loved to brag about their wealth, the trips they had taken, and the lucrative business deals they had made.

After a few drinks, we climbed onto the couple's boat and headed out toward the open water. It was a typically humid day, several motorboats were out, and the passengers were enjoying the sunshine. Blending right in with the Miami elite, we headed to another bar for more drinks and to meet up with more of Brent's friends.

As the afternoon wore on, I noticed that, before I finished my drink, Brent would order me another. Usually my dates asked me if I wanted another drink. Apparently Brent wanted me to know that money was not a problem for him; I assumed he was simply showing off. And, stupid me, in my nervousness, I kept drinking. Soon it was three o'clock in the afternoon, and we had still not eaten lunch. The alcohol was definitely getting to me. I found it difficult to keep my composure and not act too drunk. But, hot, thirsty, and nervous, I kept drinking, and by the time we ate lunch, I was too far gone to remember where we ate or what I ordered.

As the sun set, we drove back to Brent's place to change and freshen up for the dinner party. I stumbled into his bathroom to freshen up and stared at my disheveled reflection in the mirror. Admonishing myself for my lack of self-control, I determined I would not drink any more alcohol. *I need to sober up for the drive home. If only I were sober now, I'd make up an excuse and head home.* For me this date was over: I felt no physical or emotional attraction to Brent at all. We just didn't click, and his bragging got on my nerves. Rachel had picked Mr. Wrong. *What was she thinking? If I can just make it through dinner, then hopefully I'll be able to drive myself home safely.*

One of Brent's friends was hosting a party in a luxurious house right on the ocean. It was one of the nicest homes I'd ever been in. It was absolutely gorgeous! As Brent gave me a tour (yes, once again showing off!), I noticed the coffee table with its several lines of cocaine, my long-lost love. For three months I had avoided this white powder, but having it so generously offered, I just couldn't refuse. *Besides*, I reasoned, *the cocaine would help sober me up for my long drive home.*

I bit my lip, told myself that one line couldn't hurt, and accepted the straw that was handed to me. I snorted a line and felt a wonderful surge of energy course through my veins and wake me from my alcohol-induced stupor. I'd forgotten how good cocaine made me feel, and I foolishly accepted another line. Before I knew it, I was flying high. I was wide awake, and I felt as if I had everything under control. I was enjoying great conversations with Brent's well-off friends, and I had endless amounts of coke at my fingertips! Hours flew by.

When dinner was served, I wasn't very hungry. I ate only a few bites before we headed to the first of several nightclubs. With cocaine flowing through my body, I felt on top of the world. Confident that I was the best, most attractive person in the room, I was talking intelligently, impressing those around me, and enjoying this opportunity to party with the rich and dance at the most lavish clubs in Miami. And I totally lost track of time. Then I suddenly remembered the long drive ahead of me. *I won't have a problem driving home tonight. I got this! No problem at all!*

By the time Brent and I arrived back at his condo, it was late. I knew I didn't have the energy or the ability to drive home. I just wanted to crawl into his guest bed and sleep it off, but Brent had other plans. He stepped toward me and pushed me onto the couch.

"Get off me!" I yelled. My high was fading, and the horrible reality of what Brent was doing was sinking in. I tried to push him away from me, but he wouldn't let up. I struggled and began crying as he pulled at my clothes.

"Stop crying!" he bellowed in a cold, steely voice. The friendly Brent was gone; a powerful and threatening man had taken his place.

I froze, petrified. I knew he could really hurt me! Rage was in his voice and violence in his touch. He pinned me down, overpowering me. Terrified, I willed myself to just give in and let him have his way. If I didn't, if I tried to fight him, his rage might escalate.

Afterward I lay there, emotionally bruised, trying to fight the nausea that threatened to overtake me. Brent rolled away, but I didn't move. I hoped he would fall asleep so I could just grab my car keys and get out of there. Then I'd be okay—but for the life of me, I couldn't remember where I'd put my keys. All the drugs and alcohol blurred my thinking, and I prayed that God would get me home safely and soon.

Thoroughly exhausted, I finally fell into a restless sleep. I knew that was the only way I would sober up. When I woke, my mind was clearer. I quietly gathered my things, hoping not to wake Brent. A headache pounded in my temples, I felt sick to my stomach, and I wanted to get as far away as possible from this repulsive man. On the verge of tears, I searched for my keys. I wanted to leave right away; I didn't want to talk to Brent! I couldn't find all of my things, but at that point I didn't care! I just wanted out of there!

Suddenly I heard the bathroom door shut. *Oh, great! He's up.* Brent walked into the room where I was gathering my things. He smiled at me as if nothing had happened and asked if I'd like to go out to brunch with him. Afraid that I'd again see his nasty side if I said the wrong thing, I forced myself to smile and cautiously declined his offer, telling him I needed to get back home. Finding my keys and forcing a fake smile, I said good-bye and rushed out the door to my car. Relief overwhelmed me the moment I was safely locked in my vehicle. Then, with hot, angry tears pouring down my face, I sped out of there as fast as I could. This loathsome human being had set me up—and he probably did this to all his dates! My stomach churned as I thought about what had happened to me. I had been raped....

$\smile$

I cried all the way home, haunted by images from the previous night. I tried to push them out of my mind. What I remembered was bad enough, but I feared what I couldn't remember! Too much of the evening was a blur! Totally disgusted by the way I had acted, I was angry with myself for not having more control, for not staying away from the alcohol and cocaine. And I should never have gone on this date in the first place. *What had I been thinking? How could I have been so foolish?*

Tears ran down my face as I realized that, instead of a rich, wonderful man who would make my life complete, I'd been with a selfish, cruel man who left me with long-lasting emotional scars. Feeling dirty through and through, I wanted to hurry home, climb into the shower, and scrub myself clean. *If I could only wash away the last twenty-four hours completely... If only I could wash away the guilt that's eating away at me...* Blaming myself for getting into that situation, I was carrying a heavy burden of guilt. I just wanted the whole awful experience wiped from my memory for good.

$\smile$

That's when my friend Joe's words came to mind: "Chrissie, you're playing a dangerous game." It suddenly occurred to me that I had never once consulted God about going on this blind date. I'd had some serious reservations, but I'd ignored those concerns. Instead, I'd plunged ahead, still independently doing my own thing. Tears poured down my cheeks. I had always thought I knew what was best—and I wanted to be in control of my life. So not for a second had I considered praying about whether or not to go on this date. Instead I had trusted Rachel's advice rather than paying attention to the red flags God had quietly planted in an effort to get my attention.

I realized—and it was like a dagger in my heart—that I had turned away from God, from the One who truly loved me. He was the One who wanted to protect me and who could protect me, and I hadn't even thought about

Him when I was considering making plans with Brent. I also realized that if I continued living like this, I might end up dead. Joe was absolutely right: I was playing a dangerous game. I had put God in a box, and I took Him out only when I thought I needed Him. *Had I been living with Jesus as Lord, I would have spared myself this whole tragic experience....*

By the time I reached the safety of my home, I knew exactly what I needed to do. I was sick of living my life on my own. I knew that I absolutely needed Jesus to save me from myself, from my selfish and stupid way of thinking that I always knew what was right. I was thoroughly convinced that if I kept living my life my way, things would only get worse. Entering my bedroom and closing the door, I grabbed my Bible and pulled out the little booklet Joe had given me. Bowing my head, I prayed the prayer of salvation: *Lord Jesus, I am a sinner and I need You. Thank You for dying on the cross, forgiving my sins, and giving me eternal life. I open the door of my heart and receive You as my Lord and Savior. Take control of my life and make me the kind of person You want me to be. Amen.*

A sense of relief overwhelmed me. God had been knocking at the door of my heart, and I had finally invited Him in (**Revelation 3:20**). I took my one foot out of the world, and now I had both feet into the boat with Jesus: I would now trust Him to guide me. I found great peace in the wonderful promise from **John 3:16** (NASB): ***For God so loved the world, that He gave His only begotten Son, that whoever believes in Him shall not perish, but have eternal life.*** I also had something wonderful to look forward to: one day I would live in heaven, a far better place than earth—and I would live there for eternity.

As the months went by, I realized that God truly loved me despite all my mistakes, poor choices, and sin. In the world I had experienced all kinds of rejection and hurt. People I had trusted had led me astray, telling me they loved me but treating me otherwise. But God—He *loved* me! He really loved me, and He had a special plan for my life. He knew what was best for me, not in some harsh military-rule style, but in a loving Father-Knows-Best way.

For the first time in my life, I realized that God was on my side, fighting for me, protecting me, and guiding me. I was relieved that I was in the boat with Jesus. I was no longer playing the dangerous game.

Chapter 8

A New Me

Exactly as He promises in His Word, God miraculously began transforming my life, giving me a new mind and letting me see people and situations from His perspective. I wanted to walk in His ways, listen to His still small voice, and obey Him. As I read the Bible, I began to learn how to live—how to live God's way, not my way. And instead of shopping for the latest hot looks, I shopped for a church that would best fit me, one with contemporary music and where a lot of young people worshipped. During a few Sunday visits to one particular church, each sermon touched my heart, and I learned how to directly apply the teachings to my life. I joined the church and, as a new believer in Christ, continued to soak in all this valuable knowledge. Also as God has promised—and without my even noticing—my old nature gradually disappeared as I consistently attended the worship services and Bible studies.

But at first attending Bible study wasn't easy. I was nervous about meeting other Christians. *Would they judge me because of my past?* I wondered. Never having attended a College and Career Bible Study, I worried about how the group would receive me the first time I went. Surprisingly, they accepted me with open arms, and they were excited to hear about my experience with God. I was shocked by their reaction: they honestly wanted to hear every detail! Not only that, but people my age were praying for me and encouraging me every week. With their support, I was winning the battle against any temptation to fall back into my old ways.

I was still living at home with my parents and still teaching aerobics at the health club. And for the first time in my life, my mother opened up: she told me about her relationship with God and her struggles, things I had never known about her. If people had told me that my mom and I would be talking to each other like this one day, that we would become friends, I would have said they were crazy, but it actually happened. I started listening to her advice and suggestions.

I also returned to school as a full-time student, and I was blessed to have my parents' financial support—with one stipulation: that I earned at least a B average. Well, I did better than that! I started getting As. Yes! College was much easier now than it had been, and I can't explain why. One reason, though: college was now a priority. I was embarrassed that I'd been attending the same two-year junior college for five years, so my first goal was to get my AA degree—and get it fast! I regretted the fact that partying had robbed me of some valuable years. I had, for instance, changed my major several times, not knowing which direction to go in. But now, with guidance from God and from my parents, I chose to go the physical education route. I had clear goals and a new passion for achieving them. I was determined to stay focused on my relationship with God. I wanted to learn more about Him at church and Bible study. I also wanted to finish my AA at the community college I'd been attending and then go on to a four-year college.

As God continued to remove the blinders from my eyes, I realized that what I had found exciting in the past was no longer at all enjoyable. One evening, for instance, I was in an aerobics contest for work at a nightclub where I used to party. As I watched everyone drinking at the bar, the entire scene looked so different to me with my new spiritual eyes. This time I saw the wretched condition of the souls around me: I saw miserable people drowning their problems in alcohol just as I had previously done. Their vacant eyes reflected the brokenness they struggled with and the hurt they desperately tried to hide—and to numb. I was thankful and relieved to no longer be a part of that scene.

Also, relationships that were once significant to me were no longer important. Nor was getting drunk and doing drugs. Friends from my past faded when I explained to them my new focus in life. I never pushed

God on any of them; I simply shared how I'd realized that God loved me and had a better plan for my life than I'd been working out on my own. At first, I was lonely, but when I prayed for some Christian friends, that all changed.

One day I was working out on a StairMaster at the club when two Christian guys recognized me from school, came up, and introduced themselves. Instantly, my thick protective wall was up: I was very uncomfortable with how friendly they were! Even though they claimed to be Christians, I really wanted them to leave me alone. Beau and Doug tried to strike up a conversation, but I didn't want to waste my time. Besides, I was afraid they were only interested in physical favors, something I no longer wanted to give away. When they invited me to lunch, I declined the invitation and walked away.

The next day at school, though, Doug sat directly in front of me, turned around, and smiled "hello" at me. After class he persisted in getting to know me, and over time I realized that he and his brother were genuine, that they had no hidden agenda. I admit, I was more than a bit uneasy about becoming friends with men—and I did wonder what God was thinking! *I guess I should have been more specific when I prayed*, I thought to myself.

Clearly, bitterness from my past still affected my outlook on life: I didn't trust men, even those who claimed to be Christians. So having male friends seemed like a totally bad idea, but God knew exactly what I needed. He had good reasons for letting Doug and Beau into my life. Always available with godly advice, they encouraged me, and God used them to help heal the pain from my past involvement with men. I hated and resented men; in my mind, they were thoroughly evil creatures. But God graciously showed me through Beau and Doug that not all guys are selfish, dishonest, manipulative, and cruel. These two men were really considerate and genuinely nice, and they respected me as a person—and I wasn't used to any of that!

One afternoon, though, Doug and Beau confronted me about my behavior toward men: "Chrissie, do realize that you're known as the girl who hates men?" I was surprised to learn that. I had no idea that I was coming across as a man-hater. That's when Beau shared with me some truths about forgiveness.

But choosing to forgive was a tough assignment. The seed of bitterness, sown years earlier, had grown into a strong tree with deep roots. I was convinced—and I felt protected by this conviction—that men didn't deserve my forgiveness. Struggling to let go of and move on from all the hurt and pain, I had stuffed those feelings of rejection and unworthiness deep down, yet those feelings fueled rude behavior that would often rear its ugly head. Any man who crossed my path, looked at me inappropriately, or said anything improper got a piece of my mind. My mouth was instantly out of control. Curse words spewed forth as I verbally chopped him to pieces. He'd regret ever even looking my way—I made sure of that!

Yet now my buddies were insisting that I needed to forgive those men who had used me and hurt me just as God had forgiven me. "Men are only humans with a sin problem," they explained. Deep down, I knew that what they were saying was true. And I was no better than those men; all of us were sinners. Beau suggested I picture my former boyfriends, who had treated me like trash, as blind and lost sheep, not knowing what they were doing to me or to themselves. Beau's wise words helped me see the men in my past as God saw them. The truth was, God loved them and wanted to save them just as He loved me and had saved me.

As hard as it was for me to do, I started praying for each of those men who had used me, lied to me, hurt me, and discarded me. I will be honest: for a long time as I prayed, my feelings didn't line up with my efforts to forgive. I told God how much I hated those men and how passionately I wanted them to be punished and to pay for what they did to me. I wanted them to suffer!

Yet, as I prayed for their salvation, God slowly began cutting way at that tree of bitterness; He softened my heart and gave me a new attitude toward men. God used Beau and Doug in this healing process, and I am profoundly grateful that He brought them into my life, that He used them to deliver me from the bitterness and resentment rooted in my past. My behavior toward men needed to change, and it slowly did as my heart healed.

God not only transformed me inwardly, but He also filled my life with laughter. I found myself thoroughly enjoying life—sober. I had believed for so long that if I became a Christian, my life would be boring. Boring? Not at all! I had been so wrong, and I realized fairly quickly that there is so much more to life than getting wasted! I also really liked living without regrets and hangover headaches after an evening with my two buddies. That was great!

Also, the new me was no longer looking for a man to fulfill all my needs. You could say that, in a sense, I was dating Jesus. Spending time with Him filled the void that I had once filled with worldly possessions, including men.

I had long dreamed of having someone love me just the way I was, and all that time, that Someone was God Himself. I was very grateful for the forgiveness and acceptance He had given me. Oh, I wasted many, many years looking for love in all the wrong places. I wish I had come to know God and His great love for me sooner, but a lesson I learned fairly early on was that everything—I mean every detail of my life—happens for a purpose.

Chapter 9

God's Perfect Timing

After a year of hard work and perseverance, I received my associate's degree and decided to apply to Florida State University. The hills of the northern Florida campus, with all the beautiful trees, reminded me of the Iowa college town where I grew up. This university had an excellent football team, a sport I loved, and at the beginning of each game, the mascot—an Indian on horseback—rode across the football field throwing a flaming arrow, and the crowd cheered wildly. At the age of twenty-four, I was hoping and praying that I'd be attending those football games and cheering for *my* team. I was excited, anticipating a new life and new friends as I worked toward a bachelor's degree. Of course I encountered challenges along the way....

The first hurdle was the ACT test, and this entrance exam proved to be my first obstacle. My score was low, and I wasn't admitted for the fall semester. I was disappointed, discouraged, and frustrated. I also wasn't sure I was smart enough to pursue a bachelor's degree: I felt very inadequate. But, with encouraging words from friends and family—and their prayers—I pushed on. I found a tutor, I studied hard, and I took the test a couple more times, raising my score enough to be accepted for the winter semester.

At the time, I didn't realize that God was busy working behind the scenes for me to enter FSU in His perfect time. Often He does this, allowing our plans to unfold at a slower rate than we hope for, but I have found His timing impeccable. To this day still, I sometimes forget this lesson even though I have seen over and over again how God orchestrates all things perfectly. But I'm getting ahead of myself.

I was overcome with joy when I received my acceptance letter! I could start school in January! But soon my joy turned to worry as I considered Challenge #2: how would I find a place to live and Christian roommates? Starting midyear made finding housing even more of a challenge. Most students had started school in September and were settled for the year. Also, living in the dormitory with a bunch of partying eighteen-year-olds didn't appeal to me at all—and I knew that I definitely didn't need any distractions or temptations. So I prayed, asked God for His help, and tried to leave my worries with Him.

I contacted Kim, a girl from my church who attended Florida State, to see if she needed a roommate. Unfortunately she didn't, but she promised to keep her ears open for anyone who might be looking for one. She also invited me stay with her when I drove up for registration. I thanked her—and I thanked God that at least I knew one person. Kim and I had very different personalities, but we were sisters in Christ. I knew she would help me anyway she could.

Registration day finally arrived, and I drove eight hours toward the unknown. *Would I be able to find the administration building on this huge campus all by myself?* During that long drive, fear and discouragement were my companions, telling me that I probably wouldn't succeed at this school, that I wasn't smart enough, and that I had no business even trying. At one point I seriously considered turning the car around and heading back home. But as I neared a bypass, I saw the words "God loves you" spray-painted on the concrete bridge. Tears filled my eyes. I needed that exact message at that exact moment! *God does love me, and He is watching over me. I just need to trust Him.*

When I reached the exit for the university, I took a deep breath and asked the Lord to lead me to where I needed to go. Back then there were no cell phones, no GPS, and no printed MapQuest directions to help me. But God and the directions I'd received in the mail from FSU took me to the correct building. Parking the car, I thanked God that I had arrived safely and on time. Signs and arrows pointed the way for me, and I soon reached a line of students waiting to register. Standing in line, I tried to make conversation with the couple in front of me, but they weren't interested in talking. They were too busy kissing. *Oh great…*

I stood there, feeling a little lost and alone, when suddenly a woman cut in line right in front of me. I didn't see where she'd come from. Smiling, she introduced herself. "Hi, I'm Angela," she said, shaking my hand. She acted as if she already knew me. I introduced myself, and we talked as if we were old friends. She told me about her life, sharing that a few months before her two-year-old son had passed away due to an illness. As she talked, I was inspired by both her courage and her peaceful countenance. She seemed to have incredible hope despite her tremendous loss.

Briefly, I told her a little about my situation and how I hoped to find a quiet place off campus to live with roommates closer to my age. Not sure she'd understand, I left out the fact that I was a Christian who wanted Christian roommates. Before we went our separate ways, she made several suggestions about my housing situation. I thanked her, but as the day continued and I pursued her ideas, each one was a dead end. And as each of those doors closed, that lost, hopeless feeling engulfed me again. *Okay, God, what do I do now?* Time was running out. I'd be leaving in the morning.

<hr>

Before leaving campus and going over to Kim's apartment, I decided to stop at the food court and get a soda. As I walked through the courtyard, I saw Angela sitting on a bench, reading a book. Glad to see a familiar face, I walked over to her. We talked for a few minutes, and I thanked her again for her suggestions about housing and told her that nothing had worked out. She asked for my phone number so she could call me if she heard of anyone looking for a roommate.

Writing out my name, Angela commented that I spell *Chrissie* the same way as a girl she worked with. "She's about to graduate. Hmm… Her roommates might be looking for someone. She lives with two girls in an off-campus condo. I'll see if those two have found a replacement for Chrissie yet. If they haven't, I'll give you a call," she said.

That sounds good, I thought, *but what are the chances that these girls would be Christians? Pretty much slim and none.* Again, I felt discouraged.

I knocked on the door to Kim's apartment, and she greeted me warmly. It wasn't long before she asked about my housing situation. I told her how frustrated I was that nothing had worked out so far. She encouraged me, saying she felt certain that God would provide something soon.

As Kim and I were about to leave for dinner, her phone rang. It was Angela calling with news that her friend Chrissie's roommates were still looking for someone to live there when she moved out. Angela gave me the phone number of one of the roommates. I immediately dialed Amy's number and introduced myself.

"I can't talk right now," Amy said. "I have to get to work."

Sensing that she just didn't want to be bothered with me, I sighed. "Oh, okay. Well, where do you work?"

"Campus Crusade for Christ," she answered.

Blown away, totally amazed by God's goodness, I replied, "You're a Christian! I can't believe it! I've been praying for a Christian roommate."

My response got her attention. She stopped long enough to explain that she and her roommate, Stephanie, had been praying for a Christian roommate, too. She gave me directions to their condo, and we planned to meet the next morning before I left for home. Hanging up the phone, I stood there in shock. *Wow! God is so good!* I knew He was at work here.

So I wasn't totally surprised that the next morning, when I met the girls, it was as if I had known them for years. We clicked immediately, and I had a real peace that rooming with them was exactly where God wanted me to be. He had faithfully provided. The condo was perfect and the rent, affordable. And, on top of that, Amy and Stephanie had been Christians for several years. I knew I would benefit from their maturity in the faith.

I drove home, looking forward to telling my parents how miraculously God had worked.

In January I moved in, and I felt at home right away. Amy really knew the Bible, and she taught me practical principles about living as a Christian, about living as a blessed child of God, knowing that He was in control of everything, and not needing to worry about anything. And I had just seen the truth of that in my own life: the whole time I had worried about where to live, God was—in His perfect time—busy preparing the perfect place for me. And He had put me in that specific apartment for even more reasons than I had initially realized.

One evening, I was sharing with Amy how I had come to know the Lord and telling her about my many mistakes in choosing boyfriends. I explained that my focus had changed, that now I was serious about getting my education and, even more important than college, learning what it was to walk with the Lord. I didn't need or want a boyfriend to distract me. Sensing my strong dislike of men, Amy asked if I ever wanted to get married.

I sighed. "I'd love to get married one day—but to the right man. He'd have to understand my past addictions, and he would have to be on the same page when it came to my belief in God." An odd expression crossed Amy's face, and I wondered what she was thinking....

The next day, as I looked out the kitchen window, I saw a tall, attractive man walk out of the condo next door to ours. "Who is that?" I asked Amy.

"Oh, that's our neighbor, Jay," she answered, eying me closely.

I stared at him as he climbed into his Bronco. *Now that's the type of man I'd like to marry, but he's probably not a Christian.*

As if she were reading my mind, Amy looked at me with a smile on her face and told me that Jay was a Christian and, in fact, he had come to mind the previous night while I talked about my perfect mate. She went on to explain that he struggled with a drinking problem—and that he had a girlfriend. Learning he was off limits, I went on with my day.

But a week later Jay visited our apartment to ask for prayer. He was upset: he had recently broken up with his girlfriend, and he was struggling to stay sober. When Amy introduced us, I was not impressed. He didn't have a job, he was hung over, and he looked as if he'd been run over by a truck. Hopelessness, stress, and depression were visible in the dark circles under his eyes. He looked ill, his skin was pale and gray, and he reeked of cigarette smoke and alcohol. He didn't even make eye contact when we gathered around him to pray for him.

I felt sorry for him, but a part of me was very guarded. As we prayed, though, I heard God's still, small voice tell me I was going to marry this man one day and that he would be a great man of God. Startled, I immediately questioned God: *Are You crazy? Do You see how messed up he is? You know I don't want to get hurt again. Besides, Lord, You know I'm focusing on school right now. I don't have time for a boyfriend.* I was sure I had heard wrong.

For the next few weeks, though, it seemed that everywhere I went, I ran into Jay. I went to church—and there he was, sitting two rows behind me. I went jogging—and there he was, jogging nearby. When I was getting into my car, he was climbing into his. When I carried out the trash, he was taking his out. God continued to orchestrate these odd little meetings until I finally got the message: I should let myself get to know this guy. I cautiously began talking to him every time I saw him.

We started riding to church together, and we gradually became friends. Still, I worried: Jay obviously had a serious drinking problem. At times he disappeared for several days—going on a drinking binge, isolating himself from everyone, hiding from the world—and eventually he would reemerge. Then, for a day or two, Jay's health would be shaky and his mind not too clear, but after a while the true Jay reappeared—until the next time. His failure to answer the phone or the doorbell was a sure sign that he was drinking once again, alone in the shame-filled darkness of his illness.

Since the walls of his condo were connected to ours, during those dark times I could hear him, all alone and stumbling around. I wasn't sure how to help him. All I knew to do was to pray, and that I did. I first asked God to show me how to pray for Jay, and then I asked Him to give Jay the wisdom to find a way out of his illness and the strength to get the help he obviously needed.

I also saw that the aftermath of my salvation experience was very different from Jay's. Ever since naming Jesus my Lord, I had been able to totally avoid drugs and alcohol, but Jay continued to struggle. Although Jay loved God and truly was His child, Jay struggled with his addiction. I tried to convince him to get counseling, but he thought he could break free with God's help alone. Jay didn't feel any need to go into treatment. Since he was unwilling to admit he needed outside help, I feared he would lose his life before he got the counseling he needed.

Also fueling my concern about Jay was the fact that I was falling in love with him—and I could tell he also loved me. He treated me with respect and courtesy in a way no other guy ever had. Soon we both believed that God wanted us to marry, but not until Jay overcame his drinking problem. Both of us also realized that God had placed me right next door to help motivate Jay to get healthy.

We traveled a rocky, frustrating road for six months. It got to the point where I refused to be around Jay whenever he was drunk. Anytime I smelled alcohol on his breath, I'd tell him to turn around and go home. His addiction aggravated me! I couldn't understand why he kept falling back into his drinking. My strong cravings for drugs had left after surrendering my life to Him. *Why hadn't God done the same with Jay?* I was also aggravated because whenever Jay was sober, we had a great time together, but whenever he was under the influence, I didn't like him at all!

One afternoon I went to Jay's condo because I hadn't seen or heard from him in a week. Worried that he lay dead in his bed, I walked into his kitchen and saw vomit everywhere. Then Jay stumbled in, a disheveled drunk. I told him I was glad he was alive and that I would pray for him— and then I left him to clean up his own mess. I wasn't going to help him in any way. I was angry—angry at Jay, angry as his addiction. As I walked out the door, I was fed up and not sure I'd ever be ready to see Jay again.

And God knew that my pulling away was exactly what Jay needed. In fact, the Lord gave me the wisdom and the strength to stay away from Jay. I was not to bail him out of his messes or protect him from the consequences of his behavior. My strong-willed attitude toward men served me well: I did not become an enabler, running to Jay's rescue and trying to fix him. Instead, I trusted God: I knew that He wanted me to be with a healthy man, not an alcoholic. If God wanted me to be with a healthy Jay, He would work it all out.

Then, late one night I woke to the sound of a gunshot. Whether it was real or a dream, I wasn't sure. As I jumped out of bed, God told me to pray for Jay, who had been drinking for several days. As I interceded on Jay's behalf, I realized that he was hitting the lowest point of his life, and I sensed he wanted to end it all. With tears falling and fear for him making my heart pound, I prayed a long time.

The next morning when I went over to his condo, I was relieved to see him alive. He was sitting in a chair and staring into the distance, yet his body shook uncontrollably. I'd never seen anyone look that bad. That's when Jay's best friend arrived to take him to a detox center where he could get the medical attention he so desperately needed. He looked at me in shame, not saying a word as his friend helped him to the car.

"I'll be praying for you!" I called to him.

Yet it seemed the more I prayed, the worse Jay got. Still, night after night I begged God to help him. I also wrestled with God about a question of my own: *Why, God, why did You bring this man into my life?* In spite of my doubts and confusion, God continued to give me strength; He continued to encourage me that I was on the right path.

After six months of watching him ride a roller coaster between sobriety and drinking binges, I knew I needed to give Jay an ultimatum: "Don't call me unless you're going into treatment." Within a few days of his hearing that hard-to-make statement, Jay finally decided to get help. He packed his bags and headed to a Christian treatment center in central Florida. Pleased to see him go, I knew God would take care of him. As we hugged, we both shed some tears. We didn't know what the future held.

While Jay was in treatment, I took time to look back at our relationship. With him gone, I could easily see what God had been trying to do. At times I missed Jay, but I was glad to have the time I needed to focus on school right now. Still, I marveled at God's obvious hand in our lives. That Jay and I were next-door neighbors was definitely a God thing, and that fact encouraged me to believe that He truly had a perfect plan for both of us. As I look back, twenty-one years later, I'm still amazed by God's beautiful timing: He truly made all things work perfectly together just as He promises in His Word (**Ecclesiastes 3:11; Romans 8:28**). But I'm getting ahead of myself....

Chapter 10

Living for God

For eight long months Jay was in a Christian rehabilitation program. I looked forward to each letter he sent, telling me about what God was doing in his recovery process. And despite the fact that I was busy with schoolwork, God was working on me as well....

The Christian walk is not always easy. In fact, at times it can be very discouraging, lonely and difficult and painful, so much so that I sometimes wondered if my life would ever be easy. I had walked with God enough to know how much more rewarding it was to press on *with* God than to try to manage *without* Him, so, thankfully, I was never tempted to return to my old way of life. The years when God was not in my life were far worse than any difficult day I had when God was in my life! I knew that every struggle, every obstacle, every challenge I encountered would be used by my heavenly Father to make me a better person, to make me more like Christ. My heavenly Father disciplines those He loves, and He disciplined me (**Hebrews 12:10**).

For instance, one thing I learned during this time was that I had a temper: I handled stress by screaming, yelling, and even throwing things. My roomies were much more laid-back and easygoing; they handled a crisis very differently than I did. Unleashing cuss words when things didn't go my way, I felt out of control and totally unable to manage my rage appropriately. To be honest, I thought this behavior was normal, but after seeing my roommates' reactions to my first outburst, I was embarrassed. One roommate suggested that I read **Psalm 91** out loud to help me relax, and this advice helped me immensely. Psalm 91 enabled me to put into perspective whatever had enraged me. I also realized that deep down, beneath these angry reactions, was fear. I feared not having enough money. I feared failure and rejection. I feared the future, and when events didn't go my way, I would get angry, but the cussing was masking profound fear. I was afraid, and I didn't automatically feel secure with my heavenly Father. I'd grown up with an earthly father who was always worrying and always assuming the worst, who lived life stressed out, and who had a fierce temper. How similar would my heavenly Father be? Not similar at all, I was realizing.

After that first reading of Psalm 91, whenever I felt stress morphing into anger, I grabbed my Bible and turned to it. Those rich words—quoted below from the Amplified Bible—helped me control my anger. The words and images also calmed my nerves. I would picture my heavenly Father— my infinitely strong Protector—watching over me 24/7. This truth calmed my fears, which reduced the anxiety, stress, and worry I'd been feeling.

> *He who dwells in the secret place of the Most High shall remain stable and fixed under the shadow of the Almighty [Whose power no foe can withstand].*

After reading this first verse, I pictured myself under the shadow of the mighty, the almighty, God. I had lived with a constant sense of anxiety and fear all my life since I was little. As I grew older I handled it with drugs and alcohol. Now that I was sober, if I bombed a test or didn't have money to fix my car or got sick, if I encountered any obstacle or anything that felt like a crisis, I would freak out. But this psalm reminded me that under the shadow of my great God I could "remain stable."

> *I will say of the Lord, He is my Refuge and my Fortress, my God; on Him I lean and rely, and in Him I [confidently] trust!*

> *For [then] He will deliver you from the snare of the fowler and from the deadly pestilence.*

Verses 2 and 3 reminded me to lean on God as my refuge, to confidently trust Him, to not doubt that He would deliver me from any danger.

[Then] He will cover you with His pinions, and under His wings shall you trust and find refuge; His truth and His faithfulness are a shield and a buckler.

You shall not be afraid of the terror of the night, nor of the arrow (the evil plots and slanders of the wicked) that flies by day,

Verses 4 and 5 made me think of being a scared little girl who had always wanted safety. I grew up with a father who was fearful and anxious, so I didn't ever feel secure. I wanted to picture my heavenly Father as my safe haven; I wanted to imagine myself resting in His strong, secure arms. I learned to be fearless under God's huge wings. I felt shielded from any arrows that would come across my path and protected by the inevitable storms that rage in this fallen world.

Nor of the pestilence that stalks in darkness, nor of the destruction and sudden death that surprise and lay waste at noonday.

A thousand may fall at your side, and ten thousand at your right hand, but it shall not come near you.

When I read verses 6 and 7, I stood in awe of my God's great power. Thousands and tens of thousands of people will fall victim to "the terror[s] of the night," the arrows, the pestilence, destruction, or death—but those horrible things "shall not come near [me]"! What a promise! Although these words don't specifically speak to anger, God used them to bring peace and to defuse my anger. The Spirit used these words to get me to turn from focusing on my fears and to focusing on God. I am thankful that God used this psalm to transform me: I'm glad I'm not the angry, raging, swearing person I once was.

Because you have made the Lord your refuge, and the Most High your dwelling place, There shall no evil befall you, nor any plague or calamity come near your tent.

For He will give His angels [especial] charge over you to accompany and defend and preserve you in all your ways [of obedience and service].

Verses 9 thru 11 remind me that I had made Jesus my refuge: I knew God as my dwelling place, so no evil or disease would come near me to harm me. I was not alone in any circumstances of life. God has given His angels special charge over me to help me be obedient.

> *They shall bear you up on their hands, lest you dash your foot against a stone. You shall tread upon the lion and adder; the young lion and the serpent shall you trample underfoot.*

I learned that God enables me to bear up against all those things that trouble and enrage me. When I call upon Him for help, whatever situation I find myself, He will work things out in His perfect timing and perfect way.

Psalm 91 has always given me peace, confidence, and hope—and that peace, confidence, and hope translate into calmness even when circumstances are crazy and stressful.

During this season in my life, I also learned that money and material things were way too important to me. As a college student, I didn't have a lot of money, but I still wanted to purchase nice things. Similar to what I'd experienced when I was doing drugs, I got high wearing a brand-new outfit. It made me feel important! So whenever I was depressed, I'd imagine having all the money in the world. I believed that being rich would be the solution to all my problems.

My roommate Amy struggled with this too, and one afternoon we sat at the kitchen table dreaming about winning the Publishers Clearing House prize and talking about all the things we'd be able to purchase. But in that same conversation, Amy shared something that had helped her, something I will never forget—and it changed my whole outlook on life.

Amy drew out a line with arrows at each end ←————→ and said it was God's timeline, the arrows representing eternity with Him. Then Amy took a pen and made a small dot on the timeline that represented my life on earth. Though to me my seven or eight decades might seem like a long time, to God the span of my life is just a little speck. Amy then explained that often we try to accumulate things, thinking that stuff—that nice cars, beautiful homes, pretty clothes, expensive jewelry—will make us happy. But when we die, none of these things go with us to heaven. So on earth we should not be focused on trying to accumulate as many material things as we can; we should focus on serving God.

As if reminding and encouraging herself in her own struggle, Amy asked me, "Are you going to live for God or for the dot, Chrissie? Living for God offers the biggest reward, and that's eternity with Him. If you live for the dot, all you get is the dot. When you die, all the things you worked for stay behind. There's no reward."

I sat there thinking about what she'd said. The picture definitely helped me put material things into perspective. Trying to make myself happy with perishable goods just won't work. Instead, I realized, I needed to focus on my relationship with the Lord, to learn what He wanted for my life, to obey what He taught me, and to stop worrying about temporal things. I needed to choose to trust God to supply all my needs **(Matthew 6:33-34)**. That truth was exactly what I needed to hear. "Live for God, not for the dot"—this was my new motto.

As I learned more about living for God and started living out what I learned, the rewards of doing so became more and more evident. My internship was on the horizon, and after that, a bachelor's degree would be in my hands. I couldn't believe how God had helped me accomplish those very things I once thought I'd never be able to achieve. I did my student teaching in Orange County, close to Jay's halfway house. After visiting just one weekend, I found a girl to room with. It was a perfect situation. Once again, God provided.

And what was God doing in Jay's life during this season? Jay had started back to work during the day, and he attended a Christian recovery program in the evenings. We went to the same church and developed some great friendships with other Christians. The person I had fallen in love with was returning to me as a strong and godly man. We were finally able to have normal dates without alcohol being a problem. It took me some time to trust Jay again, but gradually we had a healthy relationship.

I graduated the following January: it had taken me nine years to earn a four-year degree, but I was proud of myself. A few months after graduation, Jay and I became engaged. Jay had been clean and sober for a year. Very much in love, we had a March wedding, and I would love to say that we lived happily ever after, but that only happens in the movies. I don't want to depress anyone with that truth, but I will say that God knew exactly the man I needed to help me grow closer to Him. With the help of Christian counselors, we have sorted through a lot of painful baggage from our past, and we have learned a lot about ourselves, each other, and God in the process. God truly blessed us with wise and godly counselors to guide us. If both Jay and I hadn't known the Lord, I don't think our marriage would have survived, but by God's grace, we pressed on.

I didn't marry Prince Charming (no one does!), but I married a man who encourages me to live for the Lord, and we both seek God to help us be loving, patient, and understanding with each other. With God's help, we've been married over twenty years. Each year has gotten better than the year before, and I can honestly say that I am much more in love with Jay now than I was on the day I married him. We've been through both bad times and good times, yet God has remained faithful. We have been blessed with a daughter whom we dearly love. At the time of this writing, Jay is CEO of the Phoenix Rescue Mission helping those homeless and struggling with addictions. I realize now why Jay had taken the path he did during his recovery, gaining valuable knowledge and wisdom he needed to fulfill God's purpose for his life. For the past seventeen years I have also been able to minister to people in the programs my husband has overseen. It has been very rewarding to see God changing the lives of those in crisis.

As I look back over my life, I am grateful for everything that happened to me along that painful road for I am able to have compassion with those hurting. I am thankful for those who prayed for me when I was lost, looking for love in all the wrong places. And I thank God that He enabled me to hear Him: I could have missed everything He had for me if, on that day the voice spoke, I had turned away and refused to listen. I never imagined being where I am today, but God had bigger and far better plans than I could have asked or imagined. He really is the love I was looking for all along, and I am so glad I found Him!

Five Lies I Believed

Part II

Becoming a Christian Will Make My Life Miserable

Little did I know that a fierce spiritual battle was raging while I was considering becoming a Christian....

I was hardheaded, and I was pushing God away. I really thought what the world had to offer would bring me true happiness. And the idea of giving my whole life over to God gave me anxiety: I thought I'd lose my friends and end up poor, miserable, and alone for the rest of my life.

When I was growing up, none of my close friends attended church on Sundays, so I felt like the weirdo. And when I did go to church, it was a boring place where only nerds and judgmental, Krispy Kreme Christians, acting holier than anyone else, hung out. My definition of a Krispy Kreme Christian is someone who appears to have lived a perfect life in a bubble where nothing has ever gone wrong, and they gaze out from their bubble to judge those who do not meet their standards. These stereotypes I developed about churchgoers started at a young age. For years, I avoided Christians— and I knew I never wanted to become one!

So, stubbornly not wanting to give up either my friends or my way of life, I searched for love in all the wrong places. Only when all my dreams came crashing down around me, only when I was sick and tired of the results of my own efforts, did I sense God gently leading me to Him. God continued to tug at my heart, and I found that my long-held views about Christians were all wrong. In fact, I wish I had known the truths that we'll discuss in this chapter much, much earlier in my life. Unfortunately, my believing the lie that becoming a Christian would make my life miserable led me down a path of wasted years that I would long regret.

The Truth Is...
Hanging out with other believers is a blessing.

Let us consider and give attentive, continuous care to watching over one another, studying how we may stir up (stimulate and incite) to love and helpful deeds and noble activities,

Not forsaking or neglecting to assemble together [as believers], as is the habit of some people, but admonishing (warning, urging, and encouraging) one another, and all the more faithfully as you see the day approaching. — Hebrews 10:24-25

When I plugged into an active and healthy congregation of believers and got to know some of them, I found that a church is a lot like a family. Some members I really liked and wanted to get to know better; others I didn't care for as much. That's the way it is with a family by blood, but there's more to the family of God. Fellowship with other believers is like being touched by God: He gives us, His children, hugs and He speaks words of encouragement through other believers. God shows us His love through His children. Many times I have had a sister in Christ say the very thing I needed to hear to lift my spirits. My brothers and sisters in Christ are blessings in my life, giving me the encouragement and prayer support I longed for and needed.

But none of us is perfect; each of us has flaws and imperfections. So, yes, at times a member of my church has hurt my feelings. It happens to all of us. But I have come to realize everyone is in the process of transformation into a more Christlike person—and each one is at a different spot. I know, for instance, that I haven't always demonstrated compassion and kindness. I am a work in progress, learning to forgive others and give them the kind of grace I need them to extend to me.

So, if you have visited a church and found people looking down on the unworthy ones who have dared entered *their* church building, you may be at the wrong church. I visited several churches until I found a church that felt like home. So don't give up on your quest to find a church family, but also remember there is no perfect church out there. But I believe God has a church family—a perfect church family—just for you. Pray, listen for God's guidance, look at some websites, visit a handful of churches. God knows how important His people are to one another: He wants you in a church family even more than you do!

The Truth Is...
God gives us the desires of our heart.

> **Delight yourself in the LORD,**
> **And He will give you the desires of your heart.**
> **Commit your way to the LORD,**
> **Trust also in Him, and He will do it. — Psalm 37:4-5 NASB**

When I first went back at church after hearing the voice, I was afraid God would either want me to become a nun or send me off to some foreign country as a missionary. My greatest fear was that God would require me to do something I'd hate. Nothing could be further from the truth. In fact, God's Word tells us that when we commit our ways to Him, when we delight ourselves in Him, He will give us the desires of our heart (Psalm 37:4-5)—and that's a tricky verse. I'll explain what I believe.

When we are walking through life with God as our focus—with the desire to obey Him, serve Him, love Him, and know Him better—He gives us the desires of our heart in the sense that He places the desires in our heart that He wants us to have—and then He fulfills them. It's not that God gives His children everything we want whenever we ask. That's not what "giving us the desires of our heart" means. So I prayed for what I thought I needed and what I wanted, but God's answer wasn't always a prompt yes to my request. So I learned to trust God: I chose to believe that He knows me better than I know myself and that He has a perfect plan for my life. I laid at His feet my goal to finish college, and I chose to trust Him to help me live in a way that pleases and honors the Lord. God was faithful, and He gave me strength to press on even when obstacles arose.

Before becoming a Christian, I made all the important decisions in life on my own—and I felt completely lost. During my first two years of college, I changed my major three times. Obviously I was confused. I wanted a career, but I didn't know which career, so I was spinning in all different directions. Baffled about my future, I spent five years at a two-year community college. That wasn't the best use of my time, but I didn't know which way to go. Fortunately, after becoming a Christian—after entering into a personal relationship with Jesus—I began to rethink what I really did desire. After much prayer and some good advice from family, I chose a major. Then I needed to sit back and relax, let God drive, and choose to trust Him to guide me, protect me, and help me.

When I look back, I see what a truly scary road I was walking. If I continued my journey in life without God leading, my path may have seemed golden and full of wonderful opportunities, but the enemy was guiding me. All the glitz and glamour had been only a façade covering my broken, empty life. Acquiring material things, having relationships with rich men, pursuing outward beauty—that was pretty much my plan for my future, and it was a plan I hoped would fulfill all my desires to be loved and accepted. But instead of having those expected and longed-for benefits, my way of life had dangerous consequences, like drug addiction, physical and emotional abuse, heartache, and further rejection.

The Truth Is...
Being a Christian means receiving many blessings.

> *"Peace I leave with you; my peace I give you. I do not give to you as the world gives. Do not let your hearts be troubled and do not be afraid."*— *John 14:27 NIV1984*

I worried that if I gave my heart to Jesus, I'd lose my any chance of seeing my dreams fulfilled—specifically, my dreams of a rich husband whose love would make me complete, who would shower me with material gifts, and who would be the key to my happiness and contentment. (What unrealistic expectations!) I also feared that, by becoming a Christian, I'd lose all that the world had to offer. And I didn't see any Christians I admired or wanted to be like, and not one of my friends was a Christian. So, yes, I'd lose all my friends—and drinking and dancing at the clubs with them.

In reality, though, when I became a Christian, I gained a life of peace I never knew was possible. Learning to cast all my cares on Jesus and to trust Him with my future brought comfort to my soul. I felt like I was free to do whatever I wanted; I've never felt like God was depriving me of anything. He worked on me very gradually, slowly changing my heart and giving me the courage to say no to my old behaviors. God has been faithful to guide me down a path of contentment. I could go on and on listing the great blessings of knowing God and being one of His kids. But I am only going to share some of the benefits most important to me.

First of all, once I really believed these important truths deep down in my heart, my life started changing. I became more confident and secure in who I was as a woman. Having total security in God's love for me, I was able to step out and do things I never thought I could do. I didn't need to care about what others thought of me; I didn't need to worry about being rejected. The one truth that mattered was that God loves me—and nothing could change that.

The Truth Is…
I am totally loved and accepted by God.

> *For I am persuaded beyond doubt (am sure) that neither death nor life, nor angels nor principalities, nor things impending and threatening nor things to come, nor powers,*
>
> *Nor height nor depth, nor anything else in all creation will be able to separate us from the love of God which is in Christ Jesus our Lord. — Romans 8:38-39*

Nothing can separate me from the love of God. Even when I screw up and make mistakes (and I do that often!), God pours out His love and forgiveness. But this doesn't mean I can do whatever I want, with the attitude of "Oh, well. God will forgive me. I don't need to worry." No! Instead I stand in awe of His total acceptance of me, and I want to do my best to please Him. God knows each one of my struggles and weaknesses, yet He is patient as He slowly transforms me into a better and more Christlike person.

Knowing that God totally accepts me not only relieves me of any pressure to be perfect, but it also gives me the confidence to press on and not give up. I will never be perfect, yet God still accepts me. In the world, however, I thought I had to be faultless in every way in order to gain approval. Striving for perfection is an unachievable goal, and all my efforts were rewarded with rejection.

And being rejected by men in the world, I feared that other believers and even God Himself could not truly accept me. It was hard for me to grasp why God would love me or forgive me when people around me had not. God's love was like nothing I had ever known. Great was His mercy toward me, and His love for me just blew my mind! Yet days would come along when I would doubt His love for me, and then I would read **Psalm 103:11-12** out loud in my room. With those rich words of truth, I had to choose to believe those words over my feelings of doubt, and then I felt an inner strength and peace. I had to believe God's loving- kindness and mercy toward me was huge! (As the heavens are high about the earth)

> *For as the heavens are high above the earth, so great are His mercy and loving-kindness toward those who reverently and worshipfully fear Him.*

> *As far as the east is from the west, so far has He removed our transgressions from us. — Psalm 103:11-12*

When I asked Jesus to come into my life, to forgive my sins, to become my Lord and Savior, several wonderful things happened. God threw all my sins away, taking them away from me as far as the east is from the west. The Holy Spirit came to me, helping me to live the way God wants me to live, showing me the way, and giving me great joy and comfort in the midst of some really tough circumstances. Yes, certain aspects my life did change. God, who is a very patient and sensitive teacher, gradually revealed to me what I needed to work on—and then He helped me make those changes.

I'm not saying that the Christian life is easy. At times in the beginning, I was really lonely, but God was faithful to replace old friends with better friends. And then I had those bad, really bad days when everything went wrong, and I wondered what God was doing and if in fact He had left me. But God used those tough situations to teach me to press on no matter what and to trust that He deeply loves me and will never forsake me.

The Truth Is...
I am secure because I am a child of God.

> *Let your character or moral disposition be free from love of money [including greed, avarice, lust, and craving for earthly possessions] and be satisfied with your present [circumstances and with what you have]; for He [God] Himself has said, I will not in any way fail you nor [give you up nor leave you without support. [I will] not, [I will] not, [I will] not in any degree leave you helpless nor forsake nor [let [you] down (relax My hold on you)! Assuredly not!*
>
> *So we take comfort and are encouraged and confidently and boldly say, The Lord is my Helper; I will not be seized with alarm [I will not fear or dread or be terrified]. What can man do to me? — Hebrews 13:5-6*

In this brief passage, God repeats "I will not" three times: He is reassuring us that He has a tight hold on us. I do not need to be filled with worry, fear, or dread of what people can do to me; God will not fail me in any way. Also contributing to my being content and satisfied with my circumstances was that—because of God's transforming touch—I wasn't craving earthly possessions the way I had been. And I believed I was secure in God's hands, that He would never leave me without His support, so my fear of being left helpless disappeared. God also healed my heart, crushed by rejection from family, friends, and those men who had professed their love for me. In the past I had spent a lot of time thinking that something had to be wrong with me!

Well, of course there's something—a lot of things—wrong with me (and wrong with you) because we're all sinners. But one thing that was really wrong with me was that I was living my life on my own: I was doing whatever I wanted without any idea I was allowing the enemy to steal from me everlasting life, a relationship with God, and peace that comes when I trust in His plans for me. God patiently waited and watched me as I looked for love and acceptance in all the wrong places. Then, in His perfect timing, He reached out to me and spoke these words: "It's time you believe: it's God." Yes, it was time for me to believe God, to turn to Him and receive His love. That was the one thing I was missing: He would fill every void and meet my every need for love, acceptance, security, and purpose in life. But, fearful and unwilling to surrender to God's friendship and guidance, I continued to look for security in the things of this world. Finally, after one of the worst nights of my life, when I was twenty-three, I surrendered my efforts to run my life; I asked Jesus to be my Savior and to save me from myself.

Is it time for you to believe that it is God who has everything you need and want? The lie that I believed—the lie that God would make my life miserable—was one way the devil tried to keep me trapped in a life of unhappiness, confusion, broken dreams, heartache, and pain. I lost years because I'd been deceived by the enemy. Don't let one more day like that go by in your life. It's time you believe, it's God. He is the only One who can heal your pain, mend your broken heart, and give you the kind of love and acceptance that you've never known—and that you can never know except from God.

> *Who is among you who [reverently] fears the Lord, who obeys the voice of His Servant, yet who walks in darkness and deep trouble and has no shining splendor [in his heart]? Let him rely on, trust in, and be confident in the name of the Lord, and let him lean upon and be supported by his God.*
>
> *Behold, all you [enemies of your own selves] who attempt to kindle your own fires [and work out your own plans of salvation], who surround and gird yourselves with momentary sparks, darts, and firebrands that you set aflame! — walk by the light of your self-made fire and of the sparks that you have kindled [for yourself, if you will]! But this shall you have from My hand: you shall lie down in grief and in torment. — Isaiah 50:10-11*

Do you hear God's voice calling you into a personal relationship with Him? Are you walking in darkness and—if you were honest with yourself— finding yourself in deep trouble and perhaps headed for deeper trouble?

Are you walking by the light of your self-made fire? I was. And I tried on my own to kindle my fire, and those efforts ended in grief and pain.

Learn from what I learned the hard way. Choose now—if you haven't already—to rely on, trust in, and be confident in the Lord. Lean on God and experience His never-failing presence and support. I made the best decision of my life that moment when I bowed before God. My life has not been the same since then. Just look at these blessings!

- God loves me!
- He has totally forgiven me and…
- He has enabled me to forgive myself for all the sins I've committed.
- He is continuing to change me into a person who is more like Jesus.
- God has answered prayers in ways far greater than I could have asked or imagined.
- God has given me peace.
- God showed me my purpose in life as He showed me to His purpose.

My life is in God's hands, the hands of One I can totally trust, One who loves me like no one else does or even can. I had long been looking for a man to love me unconditionally, to understand and encourage me, to offer guidance and support. I found all this and more in my Savior and Lord, Jesus Christ. He gave me a fresh start, and what God has done for me, He can do for you. He will do the same kind of renewing work in your heart and your life that He has done in mine. If you would like to make that life-changing decision and take the step of faith to trust God, you simply need to say this prayer:

Dear Heavenly Father,

I know I'm not perfect, and I have done things I deeply regret. Please forgive me for my sins and show me how to live a life that pleases You. Thank You for letting Your Son Jesus die on the cross to make a way for me to be able to live in heaven with You one day. I need You to take total control of my life, to guide me and direct me, to lead me in Your ways. Please come into my heart and be my Lord and Savior. Help me find the right church that will teach me Your Word. Help me obey the teachings and commands I find in the Bible. Again, I know I'm not perfect and I know I need a lot of work. Help me to continue to seek Your face. Open my ears that I may hear Your voice. Open my eyes that I may see what You want me to see. Open my heart that I may receive Your love and acceptance. I thank You for what You are going to do in my life. I am grateful for what You have already done on the cross. I pray all this in Jesus' name. Amen.

You just made the best decision of your life.

One more aspect of God's truth is important to mention again here. **Romans 8:28 says, "We know that in all things God works for the good of those who love him, who have been called according to his purpose" (NIV1984).** I have learned that all things God allows to happen in our life happen for a reason. God turns around what the devil intends to use to harm us; He can turn those painful circumstances and difficult experiences into blessings. To this day, the devil tries to discourage me and bring my spirits low. I have to constantly remind myself of the truths outlined in this chapter and choose to believe God's word over my stinkin thinking. And you'll find that you need to do the same.

Case in point. I faced many challenges while I was writing this book. It took five years to get it published, and at times I just wanted to give up. But I kept pressing on, fighting off those doubts one by one. I am telling you this because I want you to be prepared: when you decide to become a Christian and enter into a personal relationship with God, walking with Him takes perseverance. No matter what may happen, keep pressing on—and remember these truths.

Truths to Remember

The Truth Is... Hanging out with other believers is a blessing.
The Truth Is... God gives us the desires of our heart.
The Truth Is... Being a Christian means receiving many blessings.
The Truth Is... I am totally loved and accepted by God
The Truth Is... I am secure because I am a child of God.

Lie #2

When I Become a Perfect 10, I Will Be Happy

Ah! To be truly beautiful—what could be better? That's certainly a message the world shouts at us!

But, girls, if we find ourselves staring too much into the mirror or stepping on the scale several times a day, there's a good chance our focus is wrong and our priorities are out of balance. In eighth grade I started being preoccupied with my appearance, and that obsession continued into my twenties. I wanted to be loved, and I was convinced that if I became one of those beautiful girls, people around me would love me more.

I analyzed my looks long and hard, often judging myself with harsh, disapproving eyes. After all, I was sure that if I became that perfect ten, the man of my dreams would fall madly in love with me. He would then shower me with anything and everything my heart desired. No matter the cost, he would want to please me with expensive gifts. I thought the more perfect I became, the more precious I would appear to men.

I admired the celebrities and models on the magazine covers, and I wanted to look just like them. So I worked out twice a day, one hour in the morning on the StairMaster and an hour in the evening teaching aerobics. I starved myself. I totally avoided junk food; I ate only salad. Also, wanting to maintain my bronzed glowing skin, I made sure I scheduled time for the sun. To me, tan skin was better than pale, and I was grateful I lived in Florida where I could tan all year round. I didn't miss a single day of bronzing; on rainy days I spent some time at a tanning salon.

If my complexion had been clear, I might not have been obsessed about keeping my skin tan—or about wearing makeup. Going anywhere without makeup was totally unacceptable in my world. When I ran into the grocery store for a head of lettuce, when I went to the beach, and even when I worked out, I wore makeup. I never—I mean *never*—took off my makeup when I was around my boyfriend. I was afraid he would see all the imperfections of my skin. Sadly, I even slept with foundation on—which didn't help my acne one bit.

My battle to acquire perfect skin was hard work, requiring a lot of my time and money. I spent a lot of my hard-earned cash on the best over-the-counter products I could find, on facial scrubs and masques of every kind, on anything that promised results. I worked hard, but nothing seemed to completely clear up my skin. I was very thankful that makeup existed! I honestly don't know if I could have functioned without it!

So I was always frustrated when I looked at my reflection. I desperately wished I could somehow erase all my imperfections. If only I could, then surely I would have a faithful boyfriend, my life would be happier, and all my problems would disappear. But that idea wasn't true at all. No matter how good I looked, I always found someone else who was prettier. No matter how thin I was, I always noticed someone who was thinner. The truth was, this obsession with my appearance brought heartache and led me down a very wrong path in life.

Consider, for instance, the series of bad decisions that resulted from my believing that a perfect appearance is essential to being accepted and loved.

BAD DECISION #1

I made working on my appearance a priority over getting a college education. I was *too* busy working out—that I didn't have enough time for my schoolwork, my grades suffered greatly, and I ended up dropping out. I didn't care about school because teaching aerobics paid well—and it included a free membership at one of the city's elite health clubs. I wasn't thinking about how important a college education was for the future. I was thinking only that a hot body would get me what I needed and desired in this world. And once—thanks to that toned, bronzed, perfect body—I got that rich man I was waiting for, I wouldn't need a bachelor's degree in anything. So I invested time, money, and energy in getting that hot body. *What was I thinking?*

BAD DECISION #2

Using cocaine kept my weight down, suppressed my appetite, gave me energy, and increased my self-confidence. I thought the stuff was amazing! I was sliding into a size two pair of jeans with no problem at all. The thinner I was, the more confident I became… for a while.

Others seemed to admire my slender figure, but my boyfriend Tony was not satisfied: "You are too skinny." Those four words crushed me. My efforts to be good enough to be loved didn't seem to be working. I'd believed Tony would love me, cherish me, and be proud of me if I had a model's figure. So what *would* it take to get his love, acceptance, and loyalty?

In the meantime, little did I know how addictive this tiny amount of white powder was—or how costly it would be. I depended on Tony to provide it for me, which made me think I loved him. But was I in love with Tony or with this white powder? My addiction to cocaine clouded my judgment about the relationship. If that powerful white powder hadn't been in the picture, I might have been more likely to dump him and get off the rollercoaster of emotional abuse.

The Truth Is…
Being good-looking does not guarantee happiness.

Do you want to become a perfect ten, hoping that guys will seek you out? I know I'm not the only one who has thought—or thinks—like that. We all hear too many stories about the horrific things that girls do to themselves—plastic surgeries, eating disorders, using dangerous drugs to lose weight—to achieve this goal:. None of these efforts leads to genuine or long-lasting happiness. Yet we believe if we try hard enough to make our figures to image the models and celebrities on the cover of those magaizines, we will find fulfillment in our lives.

I've learned the hard way that our appearance is a shaky foundation for a sense of self-confidence or worth; it's a foundation that leaves us feeling anxious. For one thing, we all know that eventually our beauty will fade. So if we feel loved only because of how we look, we are destined to feel very insecure one day. And even before that, what if someone better looking comes along? Believe me, someone better looking will always come along!

Actually, women who are beautiful by the world's standards are often lonely and unhappy. Just watch *Entertainment Tonight* on television! Notice all the stories about gorgeous, talented actresses getting a divorce or suffering from a drug addiction or an eating disorder. It is shocking and tragic. Yet thinking they don't have any problems and their world is perfect, we envy these women—but our thinking is all wrong. You see, I once imagined these perfect tens living happily ever after like in the movies, but the truth is, they suffer from insecurity, loneliness, and unhappiness despite their head-turning good looks.

One more thing. If a woman attracts a guy basically because of her outward appearance, once they are married, she often experiences profound loneliness within that relationship. Then, when the man decides his trophy wife is looking a little tarnished, he simply moves on to a newer, shinier model. This pattern devastates many women.

And consider this. Recently on Facebook, I reconnected with a woman I had known in my elementary and middle-school years. She shared with me how envious she'd been of my appearance and my family life when she was growing up. I was shocked! When I told her about my awful acne problem, gaining weight in ninth grade, and living with my dysfunctional family, it was her turn to be as shocked as I had just been. I never, ever imagined anyone thinking things like this about me! If only she had known the truth about my world, maybe we would have been closer friends. Instead, she disliked me from a distance because she was jealous of an illusion.

Never judge people. Especially avoid jumping to conclusions about a girl until you really know her. Then you just may realize that her "perfect" life—the life that you had so longed for and maybe even felt jealous of—wasn't so perfect after all. The lie "If only I looked like her, then my world would be perfect" floats through our mind, but no one has a perfect life. Yet Satan tries to convince us that external beauty is the secret to finding happiness and the perfect life. This deceiver loves to lie to us like that and make us feel insecure. Don't believe him.

Four Secrets to Being Truly Beautiful

Secret #1: Take time to be with God.

Are you wondering how spending time with God will help you feel beautiful? Let me tell you that spending time with God significantly increased my sense of worth, and a young woman who is confident in the Lord is indeed very beautiful. Reading His Word daily nourished my soul, and we need to feed our souls just as we need to feed our bodies. Feasting on the Bible with its words of truth and its teachings about God's love encouraged me and filled me with the sense of being accepted that I had longed for. Cocaine increased my self-esteem for only a short time, and the next morning I felt worse about myself than before. But the feeling of confidence rooted in God's Word lasted much longer, and I continued to grow stronger each day.

When we spend time with God by reading His Word, we learn who we are in Christ. We gain knowledge of how God sees us and how much He loves us. The world will always judge us, but God loves us and accepts us unconditionally. *Unconditionally* means He accepts us just the way we are, with all our imperfections and weaknesses.

> *For God so greatly loved and dearly prized the world that He [even] gave up His only begotten (unique) Son, so that whoever believes in (trusts in, clings to, relies on) Him shall not perish (come to destruction, be lost) but have eternal (everlasting) life. — John 3:16*

God so greatly loves and dearly prizes *you* that He gave up His only begotten Son as the blood sacrifice for the forgiveness of your sins. When I first read **John 3:16** out loud to myself, I feel a greater sense of being loved than I had ever felt before. When I really understood that Jesus died for me, I stood in awe of how much He cares. Not one of my boyfriends would ever have suffered on a cross and died for me!

Also, as I came to feel more confident and secure in God's hands, I felt a lot less stressed: I wasn't worrying about my life and trying to achieve perfection. Also, as God continued to grow my confidence and sense of security in God, my outward appearance actually changed, so much so that others noticed. People started asking me what I was doing differently. As I rested in God, I apparently became more confident inside and more beautiful outside. Living God's way and in His love really works better than any drug or makeup ever did.

Secret #2: Love yourself and be positive.

If we accept who we are—if we accept the way God made us—and stop dwelling on our flaws, when we recognize the positive character qualities that God is developing in us, we will enjoy life more. When I learned to accept who God created me to be, I felt freed from trying to become perfect. When I didn't accept or love myself, I settled for shallow guys who were interested only in my looks, and I put up with a lot of abuse from them. I wish I had thought more highly of myself and had never allowed men to treat me as disrespectfully as I did.

Know this truth: God designed each of us to be beautiful in a unique, one-of-a-kind way. God fashioned every detail about us: He chose our eye color, hair color, and the shape of each feature of our face. He gave each of us individual interests, gifts, and talents. He develops our character in very personalized ways, giving us life events to mold us. Bottom line, He created each of us perfectly, according to His good plans for us. God even uses the traits we think are not good to help guide our steps. God made me the way He did for a reason, and He uses all my imperfections to perfect my internal character.

So, when we encounter an obstacle, we may need to pause and explore our options; we may need to pray and ask God what He wants to teach us about ourselves. God blessed my daughter when she did exactly that. As a young girl with flat feet, Jessie Lee found playing sports very painful physically. Always the last to be chosen for a team during gym class, she felt like an outsider; she felt as if God had messed up and made a mistake when He created her. As if the flat feet didn't cause enough agony, Jessie Lee experienced a growth spurt and found herself not only taller than most girls in her class but also dealing with curvature in her spine. Needless to say, these realities made for a rough time emotionally. The doctor suggested she take up swimming to both help her spine and take pressure off her feet. To our surprise, we learned that Jessie Lee is an excellent swimmer. During this time she also discovered her singing talent and learned that the best exercise for singers is swimming. Never would my daughter have tried swimming if God hadn't given her flat feet! I can look back and easily see how God used Jessie Lee's flat feet to direct her path.

Similarly, God used my acne for my own good. My awful acne was a major obstacle for me. I had huge blemishes on my chest, my back, and my arms, so I refused to wear many revealing outfits. I chose clothing styles that hid imperfections. If I'd had perfectly flawless skin, I know I would have dressed in skimpier, more revealing outfits. I can see now how God may have protected me from getting into more physical relations with men. Little did I know that the thing I hated most about myself was shielding me from additional heartache and relational train wrecks.

It's true: God often moves in mysterious ways. He has a plan for our lives, and His plans are for our good. God never intends to hurt us; He wants to guide us, protect us, and direct us. So, whatever we dislike about our physical appearance, we need to trust that God knew what He was doing when He formed us.

> *For I know the plans that I have for you, declares the Lord, plans for welfare and not for calamity, to give you a future and a hope. — Jeremiah 29:11 NASB*

Secret #3: Take care of the body God gave you.

God only gives us one body for this earth, so we must take care of it. As an aerobics instructor, I exercised on a regular basis, but I was starving myself (I only ate salad) and feeding my body all kinds of toxic drugs. My regular diet of cigarette smoke, alcohol, and cocaine was causing all kinds of damage to my body chemistry. If I had continued this behavior, the abuse would have started taking its steep toll. I am sure that I was already doing unseen, internal damage, and I am grateful I stopped using when I did. I had plenty of warning signs that I should have stopped before I did, but I didn't pay attention to them. My periods were irregular and the doctor suggested going on the birth control. That helped, but then I developed migraine headaches. My hormones were way out of balance.

God has designed us women with the hormone estrogen that keeps our hearts healthy and our skin young, but this blessing sometimes feels like a curse. Each month, as estrogen levels fluctuate, we feel and see the effects: acne, mood swings, headaches, and depression. Sometimes we even get a little paranoid, thinking people are talking negatively about us. Often we become too sensitive, feeling easily stressed and overtired. If we are not eating right, our diet can affect our hormones, and we might experience worse effects each month. Hormones have a lot to do with our mood and our emotions. I know because I struggled with moodiness ranging from anger to depression. I would want to isolate myself from the world when I felt especially ugly and fat. So I used drugs to get the emotional lift I needed.

What I actually needed was a nutritious diet to go along with my exercise program. Eating right helps tremendously with moodiness and depression, and daily exercise pulls us out of the doldrums and helps us mentally, physically, and even spiritually. My problem was, I was doing too much in the exercise department and not enough in the area of nutrition.

Exercise demands good nutrition, and eating healthy foods rather than junk gives us energy and stamina to face life's challenges. If we were to fill up the gas tank of our car with Coca-Cola, the car wouldn't run well. The same is true with our bodies. We need to eat healthy foods and a balanced diet so our bodies and brains will function properly. Too much refined sugar tends to lead us into sugar blues that easily turn into depression, making us sluggish both physically and emotionally. I once heard a famous model say, "Nothing tastes as good as skinny feels," but I would have to disagree. *Skinny* can mean unhealthy, weak, and sickly. "Nothing tastes as good as healthy feels" is the statement I prefer. What we eat is not about being skinny, but healthy.

And I love feeling healthy rather than skinny. When I was skinny, I felt weak and depressed, but when I am healthy, I feel strong and confident. Instead of starving myself, I've learned to eat small portions, a little from each food group. I avoid junk food, and I take a good multivitamin. These relatively simple steps have made the difference between me feeling lousy and feeling great.

Exercise is key, diet is important, and so is sleep. When I used cocaine as an energy boost, I could stay up all night, but by doing so I was robbing myself of precious sleep. On some days I got only four hours of rest if I was lucky. Our body needs to rest and recuperate each day, and resting every muscle is essential to relieving stress. No wonder I needed an energy boost each night! My body was exhausted from lack of rest, poor nutrition, and the stress of working out. After getting off drugs, I cherished my sleep. Now, I get at least eight hours of rest each night. Doing this not only helps me to think better, but perform better as well. And I don't miss at all the dark circles that were once under my eyes.

Another essential aspect of loving ourselves is to practice daily hygiene. Showering, washing our hair, brushing our teeth—these things are not acts of vanity! You may not be happy with what you have, but taking care of it is better than just letting it go.

Regular exercise, a healthy diet, adequate sleep, and good personal hygiene—all these make us feel better about ourselves, protect our overall health, and reflect how much we value the body God has given us.

Secret #4: Live a balanced life.

In the Bible God talks about living a balanced life:

> *Be well balanced (temperate, sober of mind), be vigilant and cautious at all times; for that enemy of yours, the devil, roams around like a lion roaring [in fierce hunger], seeking someone to seize upon and devour. — 1 Peter 5:8*

Living a balanced life protects us from being devoured by our enemy, the devil. "How?" you may ask.

For starters, if you spend all your time at church, reading the Bible, going to Bible studies but spend zero time working out, your physical health will suffer. If you work out all the time but never spend time with God, learning His Word, your spiritual health will suffer: you may become depressed because you are not feeding your soul. If you eat healthy foods but never work out, your body will not be strong physically. If you are regularly doing schoolwork into the early-morning hours, not sleeping well, eating junk food, and not exercising, you become a highly educated person, but you won't be a healthy educated person—and you won't be able to achieve that career goal if you're lying in bed exhausted and sick suffering from a disease. Too much of any one thing isn't good. Got it? Good!

Living a balanced life is simple to outline, but I do understand it's not necessarily easy to do. Planning to live a balanced life is an important first step, though. I schedule my day so that I'm spending a little bit of time working on each different area. I spend time with God and spend time with my family. I try not to spend too much time on the computer or watching TV. I schedule time to work out and time to do daily chores around the house. I try not to eat the same thing every day. I mix it up a little. Do you realize if you eat too much of the same food your body can suffer? You need foods from all the food groups—and a little junk food here and there isn't too bad either.

Balance out meeting your physical, spiritual, and educational goals—and don't stress out because you want to be perfect. Striving to be that perfect ten can only bring heartache, frustration, and unhappiness. I know: I tried to reach that goal for years. Don't waste your time pursuing the lie. Instead invest your time in the four secrets of being truly beautiful. As **1 Peter 5:8** says, *the enemy will seek someone to seize upon and devour.* That someone will be a person whose life is out of balance in some way. So stay balanced—and don't forget these four secrets:

Four Secrets to Being Truly Beautiful

Secret #1: Take time to be with God.
Secret # 2: Love yourself and be positive.
Secret #3: Take care of the body God gave you.
Secret #4: Live a balanced life.

My Parents Are Out to Ruin My Life

During my teenage years, I began to wonder if my parents really loved me. They never seemed to understand what I was going through, so I never really had a relationship with them. I rarely shared my feelings with either my dad or my mom; I just kept to myself. And when I was fifteen, I was convinced that my parents were out to ruin my life. So I ignored their advice and instead listened to the opinions of my friends.

My mom and dad had no idea of the pressures I faced—at least that's what I thought. I wanted to fit in with the world, I wanted to have money, and I wanted to be popular. And—I believed—if I were their perfectly obedient daughter, who followed all their rules, I wouldn't have fit in. But were they really trying to ruin my life? Let's answer that question by looking at some of the lessons my parents tried to teach me. I heard these wise words preached over and over, but they went in one ear and out the other. I never took my parents or their advice seriously—but I truly wish I had.

My Parents' Advice

1. **Go to church regularly.**
2. **Do your best in school and get a college education.**
3. **Work hard and save your money.**
4. **Do not have sex before marriage.**

Instead of appreciating these solid guidelines for life and following them, I chose to believe that living according to their recommendations would keep me from reaching my goals in life. **So I chose to do completely the opposite of what they said.**

1. **I avoided church as much as possible.**
2. **Getting a college education was last on my list of priorities.**
3. **I did work hard teaching aerobics and waitressing, but I didn't put aside any money in savings. Instead I spent what I earned on whatever I wanted at the moment.**
4. **I tried to keep my virginity, but it wasn't as easy as I thought it would be.**

The truth is, if I had followed my mom and dad's counsel, I would have avoided a lot of heartache. My parents were sharing information vital to my well-being, but I chose to believe it was worthless advice, intended to keep me from the real world. After all, I didn't want to live my parents' lifestyle; I wanted much, much more out of life. Only after I myself became a parent were my eyes opened to some important truths. I'd like to share them with you.

The Truth Is...

No parent is perfect.

When I was very young, I tended to see my parents as flawless, because I didn't know any better. But as I grew older, I compared them to other parents. Before long their negative (from my perspective!) characteristics started to irritate me, and I reached the point of desperately wishing I had different parents. I often blamed them when I was hurting, and I remember being disappointed and frustrated that they didn't have all the answers or the ability to fix all my problems. I reacted with anger. I never considered that they were trying to give me the best guidance they could. So I developed the bad habit of shutting them out. I never shared my hurt and frustration with them, I shut down emotionally, and I stopped listening to the wisdom they had to offer.

Then I became a mother. When I gave birth to my eight-pound baby girl, the love I had for her was beyond anything I could have ever imagined. I never knew that I could love someone so much! I wanted Jessie Lee to have the best of everything, but I know that at times I have failed her. Superwoman I was not—and I'm still not! I was only a human being trying in my own strength to make her world perfect. When my daughter became a teenager, we had huge arguments; we completely aggravated with each other because of our different personalities. I had to remind myself that she was unique and that God made her in a special way for a reason. If I could have taken all her problems away with a wave of my magic wand, I would have done it. I wanted to be the perfect mother, and I felt guilty every time I messed up—which was often. Then one day a friend said, "Chrissie, if you were the perfect parent, Jessie Lee would never need a savior." Wow, she was right! If I were the perfect mother, Jessie Lee would never feel the need for a personal relationship with Jesus. He knows her better than I do. Only God can meet all of her needs. Now I know why my parents wanted me to go to church. I needed God to do for me what they couldn't do!

For the first time in my life, I realized what my parents must have been thinking and feeling when they encouraged me to go to church. They struggled to be the best parents they could be, and the pressures of this world made it even more difficult. With heartfelt compassion, I understood more clearly how difficult it was for my mom and dad to parent me, first a high-maintenance child and then a rebellious teenager.

So why can't parents be perfect? Have you ever thought about that? Imagine never disagreeing with your mother or father, feeling as if they always encouraged you exactly the right way, and being grateful that they always provided anything your heart desired. To some of us, that may sound like a dream come true. But perfect parents would not be good for us. After all, if existing under my parents' roof had been an awesome experience, I probably would never have wanted to grow up, move out, and become an independent adult. That was a good reason why we butted heads and got into arguments! I was figuring out who I was as a person, separating myself from them, and slowly gaining my independence. God designed our relationship with our parents to be imperfect for that reason: our differences encourage us to get out of the nest and start living on our own.

The Truth Is...
Parents have a lot of responsibilities, and responsibilities can bring lots of stress.

Sometimes I felt like a burden to my folks, especially when they seem stressed. I desperately wanted to be loved, but I felt that I was a bother. My mother went to college during my elementary school years. She was either studying for a test or suffering from headaches. It seemed that when I needed her, she wasn't available. At the time, when I didn't get the attention I wanted, I felt let down, but looking back now I can see that she was trying to juggle several things. With my dad traveling a lot, she was basically a single parent Monday through Friday every week. She was taking care of two kids and carrying a full load of college courses.

The truth is, both my parents were overloaded with responsibilities, and with those responsibilities came stress. They were torn in several directions as they nevertheless tried to meet everyone's needs and expectations. Although they loved me—I understand now—they were not able to always be there the way I would have liked them to be. Life in this world is far too busy, and we human beings make mistakes. Many a parent's brain is overloaded and has stopped running efficiently. Not understanding the disconnect with my parents, I concluded that they didn't love me—which wasn't the truth at all.

The Truth Is...
Parents love the way they were loved.

Without realizing it—and many, if not most, parents don't realize it—my mom and dad parented the way they were parented, and that meant they made the same mistakes their parents did. After all, a child doesn't come with an owner's manual, so it's natural for us to parent in ways that are familiar to us, and that means parenting the way we were parented and, consequently, making the same mistakes they made. Being a parent myself, I can say without exaggerating that it is absolutely the hardest job I have ever had—and, frighteningly, I have occasionally found myself acting just like my dad even though I'd vowed to never treat my kid the way my father had treated me. Yet in a stressful situation—and parenting means lots of stressful situations—we tend to fall back to what we are familiar with. Even well meaning, god-fearing mothers and fathers fail by provoking their children, losing their temper, and saying unkind things. And there are parents who learned from the ways they were parented, and they are intentional about breaking the pattern desiring to parent differently. Yet some parents haven't worked through their own traumatic, painful childhood memories and the sense of poor self-worth that resulted, and these individuals are more likely to have anger issues. I know about those….

At times when I was growing up, I'd make a suggestion that I thought was relatively insignificant and harmless, but my dad would go ballistic. Not realizing that I was inadvertently touching on the pain in his life, I'd press my point and be pushing against his old wound—and he would explode in anger. I learned years later that my dad had had a very horrible upbringing. When he was able to talk about it, I could see the hurt and pain in his eyes as he shared stories of how his father had treated him. Under the circumstances of his own upbringing, my dad was being the best father he could be. He loved me to the best of his ability. I understand that now, but at the time, all I knew was that I was being fussed at.

Maybe that's been your experience. Remember that if we look deeper at someone who is angry, we might recognize hidden pain in that person's life. Understanding that person helps lead to our healing. I know that was true for me: the more I understood about my father's pain, the more sympathetic I became and the better I could cope with his anger and criticism.

Believe that the vast majority of parents do the best they can.

The Truth Is…
It's a parent's job to offer counsel.

Yes, parents can come across as critical, but it is rarely—if ever—because they want us to feel bad. Throughout my whole life, my dad has been an expert at pointing out every single one of my flaws. He seemed to always notice what I did wrong and where I needed to improve, and he didn't seem to see me do anything right. As a result, I felt hopeless and came to the conclusion that I couldn't do anything well or right! I was pretty down on myself, but the criticism encouraged me to strive for perfection. I strongly believed that if I were a perfect ten, I would be happy. My father had no idea his interactions with me were fostering this unhealthy goal, that his parenting was hurting me instead of helping me.

Unfortunately, this lack of awareness is not uncommon among parents. Wanting to be sure their children don't make the same mistakes they did, they point out any pitfalls they see and any bumps in the road that they believe could cause even a small problem in their child's future. Often they tend to say too much, overemphasizing their concerns and seeming to constantly criticize. But really our parents are acting and speaking out of fear, love, and concern for our well-being.

The Truth Is...

God uses our parents to protect us.

My parents worried about the most ridiculous things. As a result, I couldn't do anything without them making me feel fearful. It drove me crazy—and out of the house at eighteen. Too many of their rules and restrictions were dragging me down. But the truth is God had placed my parents over me—just as He has placed your parents over you—as a shield of protection to keep me safe.

Picture a three-year-old trying to tie her shoe without success. When we attempt to help her, she screams, "I do it! No! I do it!" We look at her with frustration as she continues to struggle with her shoelaces, clearly not knowing what she is doing, but at the same time, she refuses to let us show her how it is done. When my daughter would act like this, I told her, "Hey, I'm thirty years older than you are—and don't forget it!" It was utterly ridiculous for a three-year-old to tell me what to do! I had thirty more years of wisdom and life experience than she did!

And I'm sure my parents felt the same way when I turned up my nose at their advice and acted as if they came from the dark ages and didn't know anything. One sign of maturity is to realize that we don't know everything and that we need to listen to our parents' advice. They have experienced things we have not. Of course our moms and dads sometimes seem cautious when we don't see any reason for it, but listening to their concerns might result in real blessings in our lives. I know now it would have been good for me to learn what I could from my dad and mom. I could have benefited greatly.

God, for instance, can use our parents to open and shut doors for us, to guide us in the way He wants us to go, and to choose friends wisely. But I only allowed my parents to meet a friend or boyfriend for a quick hello. I chose to hang out away from home: I never let my parents get to know the group I socialized with. Maybe if I had, my parents would have warned me about the people who were influencing me. Their insight could have been God's way of protecting me. Besides, most of my teenager friends were temporary and only looking out for themselves, but my parents' love and support have been constant. They have known me much longer than any of my friends, and their insights along the way should have been more precious to me.

> *Honor your father and mother—which is the first commandment with a promise—that it may go well with you and that you may enjoy long life on the earth. — Ephesians 6:2-3 NIV*

The Truth Is…
God handpicked our parents just for us.

I dreamed of having parents who were rich, who gave me everything I needed and anything I desired, but God had other plans for me. He knew exactly what type of people would best raise me. God handpicks our moms and dads for specific reasons. In His wisdom He uses all things in our lives, even our imperfect parents, to mold us and make us the person He wants us to be. We may completely disagree with God's choice, and we may even be flat-out angry with Him because of the pain His choice of parents caused us. Still, the truth is that God knew what experiences would best shape our character and move us along the path He has for us.

The Truth Is...
We need to take responsibility for our actions and stop blaming our parents.

One of the hardest things we can do is to take responsibility for our actions, but it is a sign of genuine maturity. By nature, we human beings want to blame someone else for our poor decisions. Our parents are the easiest targets because they're close and because, after all, they were supposed to guide us and nurture us.

I admit it: I blamed my parents for my unhappiness. I accused them of causing me to make bad decisions, and I told myself, "If my parents had been different, then I would have behaved better and my life would have been easier." But as I matured, I stopped blaming my mom and dad, and I started taking responsibility for my own actions and choices. I decided to make my life count no matter what my parents had been like. Asking God to help me forgive them and let go of the pain they had caused me was a huge step in my walk with Him. But God had shown me that He knew what was best for me and that He loved me more than my parents did. Having a relationship with my heavenly Father has helped me forgive and love my parents. God continued to enable me to give them the grace and mercy that He has given me.

The Truth Is...
Your heavenly Father loves you more than you can possibly imagine.

> *Can a woman forget her nursing child…? Yes, she may forget, yet I will not forget you. Behold, I have indelibly imprinted you on the palm of each of my hands. — Isaiah 49:15-16*

Having a mom or dad who has been physically or verbally abusive or who was dealing with a drug or alcohol addiction, a mental disorder, or a criminal history may cause you to wonder what God was thinking when He brought you into this world. You may have wished your parents had put you up for adoption—or maybe they did, and that's a source of anguish for you. Each one of us can talk about pain caused by our imperfect parents, and some stories are worse than others. But let me remind you that no one lives in an ideal family unit with perfect parents. The truth is, the vast majority of us live in a family that is, to one degree or another, dysfunctional, and each family's particular dysfunction comes with its own type of drama. And the flavor of your family drama has and does affect you and who you are today. Some of us may be very aware of the specific pain our parents caused, remembering every detail of every occurrence. Some people—consciously or unconsciously—stuff their pain down deep inside in an effort to forget the event and move on as if it had never happened. No matter how much or how little you are hurting, God can heal you. (Go ahead. Read that sentence again!)

That said, your anger toward your parents or a given situation may be totally legitimate, but be careful. Don't allow resentment or bitterness to bring you down, harden your heart, and turn you away from God. Lean into God, allow Him to heal your brokenness, and pray for His guidance and direction. Also, look back over your life and notice how God has used your parents to help develop your personality and enrich your story. God wants us to honor our parents, and He will help us to do so even if they are difficult and overbearing. And even if they are not the greatest parents in the world, we can learn from their weaknesses and mistakes.

Isaiah 49:15-16 gives us a picture of how much God loves us. (*Indelibly* means incapable of being removed, erased, or washed away.) Your mother may forget or abandon you, but God has not forgotten you. Every single one of His children is indelibly imprinted on the palms of His hands—and nothing can change that. So don't doubt God's love for a second. Your heavenly Father loves you more than you can possibly imagine.

> *Although my father and my mother have forsaken me, yet the Lord will take me up [adopt me as His child]. — Psalm 27:10*

In closing, don't believe the lie that your parents are out to ruin your life. Instead hold on to the truth that you are God's child and you are precious in His sight. He has a plan for your life, and your parents were a part of that plan. Trust that He knew what He was doing when He placed you with your parents.

Truths to Remember

The Truth Is…

No parent is perfect.

The Truth Is…

Parents have a lot of responsibilities, and responsibilities can bring lots of stress.

The Truth Is…

Parents love the way they were loved.

The Truth Is…

It's a parent's job to offer counsel.

The Truth Is…

God uses our parents to protect us.

The Truth Is…

God handpicked our parents.

The Truth Is…

We need to take responsibility for our actions and stop blaming our parents.

The Truth Is…

Your heavenly Father loves you more than you can possibly imagine.

If I Were Rich, My Life Would Be Perfect

I often imagined the day when I would be rich and famous, when everyone would know my name, when I'd be able to purchase anything without worrying about the price, when money was not a problem at all. I pictured myself hopping on jets, traveling all over the world, buying luxury automobiles, living in a lovely home with all the amenities, and vacationing in exotic places. And work? I wouldn't have to work for a living! And this—I truly believed at the time—would be the perfect life.

And believing the lie that if I were rich, my life would be perfect guided my decisions. One major reason I continued to date Carl was because he was from a wealthy family, and driving around town with him in a fancy car made me feel important. I also loved dining in expensive restaurants and lounging poolside at the country club. With Carl, I was living the rich lifestyle I had longed for. So for three years I tolerated his abuse because I was unwilling to let go of the luxuries that came with the relationship. I thought if we married, I'd be set for life, rich and with absolutely no worries. After we broke up, I missed the diamond jewelry he had given me and the perks of his lifestyle, but I didn't miss *him* one bit. I had used him, and that was wrong.

Sadly, though, my pattern continued: I only wanted to date attractive men who had money. The main reason I went on that horrible blind date with Brent was because he was rich. I hoped he would be my handsome Mr.

Right, willing to put a huge diamond ring on my finger. Well, you know how that date ended. If I hadn't believed the lie that being rich would bring me happiness, the idea of meeting Brent wouldn't have grabbed my attention as it did. All I could see were the dollar signs, so I hoped he was the handsome, rich man I'd marry, the man who would bring me true happiness.

But here's the big question: if this lifestyle of having it all is so wonderful, why do some celebrities seem so unhappy? These beautiful, rich people who, as far as we can see, don't have a care in the world sometimes commit suicide. How can anyone with such a fantastic lifestyle ever get that depressed? And who would divorce them? And why do they use drugs? Aren't they happy? They have everything a person could possibly want! Obviously they don't....

I spent a lot of my time and money on getting nice things, including a rich boyfriend to make me happy. The truth is, I was wasting my energy trying to reach a goal that, in the long run, would not bring me happiness at all. Oh, it might have given me some satisfaction for a short time, but that satisfaction wouldn't last.

Let us discuss some truths about money that I wish I had known long before I did.

The Truth Is...

Money does not buy happiness. In fact, the exact opposite may be true.

On plenty of occasions I've imagined the Publishers Clearing House people arriving at my door and handing me the first of several checks for one million dollars. Wow, that would definitely change my life! Immediately I'd think of all the things I could do with the money, how all my problems would disappear, and how I would smile through life from then on.

One day, however, I saw a television show about these so-called lucky winners. I learned a strange thing from these interviews with people who had won huge amounts of money. Almost all of them said that the money turned out to be a curse, not a blessing. The heartache resulting from the gift of free money was unbelievable. Several couples got divorced. Family members, friends, and even strangers wanting a piece of the fortune bombarded the winners. Many winners lost friends, and others became unable to tell who was a true friend. Spiteful people threatened to hurt them and their children if they didn't receive a share of the fortune. Several winners became addicted to drugs and alcohol. Others developed health problems as a result of the stress their newfound wealth caused, and, sadly, a few even lost their lives to murder, cancer, and suicide. The interviewers—and the TV audience—unexpectedly discovered that money did not increase these people's happiness; it actually led to great sorrow. Most of the winners declared that they wished they had never received their windfall, saying they had been much happier before they had all that wealth.

After watching this show, I realized that if God really wanted me to win the Publishers Clearing House sweepstakes, He would let it happen. But maybe He knew it would be a curse rather than a blessing. As I was growing in my relationship with God, I was learning more about money and about what was really important in life.

The Truth Is...
The important things in life
cannot be bought.

One morning in my Sunday school class, I was listening to the prayer requests. We prayed for friends to be healed, for marriages to be mended, for broken relationships to be restored. I realized at that moment that no amount of money can heal a marriage. We can pay for counseling that might help, but in reality, only the hand of God can change hearts. When we are sick, money helps by paying for our medical care, but doctors can only do so much. Only God can fully heal the human body because He is the One who designed it. God is able to do what man cannot, and we cannot put a price tag on what God does for us.

Money can alleviate some problems, but money can't change the big things, the important things, of life. Only God can. King Solomon put it well in **Ecclesiastes 2:10-11 (NIV1984):**

I denied myself nothing my eyes desired;

I refused my heart no pleasure.

My heart took delight in all my work,

and this was the reward for all my labor.

Yet when I surveyed all that my hands had done

and what I had toiled to achieve,

everything was meaningless, a chasing after the wind;

nothing was gained under the sun.

King Solomon learned that having nice things, having all that his heart desired, didn't matter that much in the end.

The Truth Is...
Earthly possessions are temporal.

> *"Do not lay up for yourselves treasures on earth, where moth and rust destroy, and where thieves break in and steal. But lay up for yourselves treasures in heaven, where neither moth nor rust destroy, and where thieves do not break in and steal. For where your treasure is, there will your heart be also."* — *Matthew 6:19-21 NIV1984*

Most material things here on earth don't last very long. Do you remember when flat-screen TVs first came out? Almost everyone wanted one, but few could afford it. Those who did spend the money were soon disappointed because the quality and design of this newer technology steadily improved, and the price went down. The buyers yearned to replace their inferior sets with the newer, nicer models. This is true with most high tech gadgets out there. The cycle continues, causing many to go into debt because they have to own the latest new thing around.

We can have a house full of the best of everything, stuff that cost us thousands of dollars. Then, suddenly, without warning, it can all be taken away. A storm, fire, flood, earthquake, or thief can come along and wipe away everything we own. Often when these catastrophic events occur, we realize the important "things" in our life are irreplaceable—and are not necessarily things at all. Our loved ones, our family and friends, matter most. We know we can rebuild a house and start again to gather more stuff, but we realize that our possessions are relatively unimportant. Strong, loving relationships, not our material belongings, bring true satisfaction and joy.

Whenever I focus too much on acquiring some particular item that I think will make my life better, I need to recognize that I am once again believing the lie that being rich will make me happy. Instead, I would be wise to appreciate the gifts I already have, those gifts that truly matter in this world. My family, friends, talents, and good health are only a few of those God-given blessings.

During the first three years of our marriage, Jay and I lived paycheck to paycheck, never indulging in the luxuries of eating out or vacationing as we worked our way out of debt. Slowly, our income increased, but our happiness did not. It seemed that the more money we earned, the more money we needed. And that leads to the next important truth.

The Truth Is...
No matter how much money we have, we always want more.

Too often Satan whispers, "If you had more money, think how much better your life would be." He might even suggest that if God really loved me, I'd have everything I wanted. Yes, the lie that money will bring me happiness is a thought I often find myself fighting from time to time even today.

When I was first learning this truth, God was definitely providing for my needs, but deep in my heart I was never really satisfied. I always wanted more. I found myself mad at God for withholding things from me, but not having all I desired really was a blessing in disguise, and it continues to be. If I had all the money in the world, I might not have taken a job or pursued a career. I also know for certain that if I'd been a rich teenager, I would have done way more drugs because I could have afforded more. God gives us what we need and what we can handle, for a specific purpose. If left on our own, we human beings would always want more.

The Truth Is...
God gives us as much money as we can handle.

> *My God shall supply all your needs according to His riches in glory in Christ Jesus. —Philippians 4:19 NIV*

The almighty Creator God—who owns everything, who made everything, who keeps the stars, the moon, the sun in the heavens and the planets in their orbits—is also in control of our income. The all-knowing, all-powerful God—who controls the ocean tides, who designed our bodies to work with intricate precision, and who gave us a mind and self-awareness—knows what we need and what is best for us. Yet if I always had everything I wanted, would I really see my need for God? And I know for myself that it's been during the financially lean times of life that I've learned the most about my heavenly Father. Those lessons came as I chose to trust Him and be patient, and believe God was working everything for my benefit.

Another important lesson I learned was to focus more on giving than receiving.

The Truth Is...
You reap what you sow.

> *"Give, and it will be given to you. A good measure, pressed down, shaken together and running over, will be poured into your lap. For with the measure you use, it will be measured to you." — Luke 6:38 NIV*

I used to complain about not having nice things, and I questioned why some of my friends had more stuff than I did. Growing up, I envied those kids who had wealthy parents and received everything their heart desired. Believing the lie that money would make my life perfect made me self-centered and selfish. As I matured, I realized that my attitude needed to change. I needed to be more of a giver than a taker; to think of others more than myself; and to see how I could help people less fortunate. Even if I don't always have money to give, I always have talents and time to invest.

In the Bible God talks a lot about money, and I learned from His Word that the more I give—the more of His blessings that I share—the more of His blessings I receive. As I sowed seeds of helping others, blessings fell in my lap. "You reap what you sow" is a truth to remember.

So treat others the way you want to be treated, and that's easier to do when you're not in love with money. The world encourages us to take and acquire and earn all that we can. Beware, the love of money leads to greed and selfishness: we think only of ourselves and what we want.

The Truth Is...
The love of money can lead us astray.

> *The love of money is a root of all evils; it is through this craving that some have been led astray and have wandered from the faith and pierced themselves through with many acute [mental] pangs.* — *1 Timothy 6:10*

Money in itself isn't inherently evil. According to the Bible, the love of money is the root of all evil. What we do with the money and how much we rely on it for our security is what can cause problems. The problem is letting money become our god, allowing it to rule our lives.

We need to be careful that we don't let a love of money lead us down the wrong road, compel us to choose a career only because of the pay and settle for a boyfriend or friends based on a their wealth, not character. Striving to be wealthy can leave us empty and feeling lost alone. Be aware that believing the lie—that money brings happiness—prompts us to wander from what is really important in life: our relationship with Jesus Christ. A relationship with Him can bring us wisdom in choosing our career, and friends that will fill us with joy that no amount of money can buy.

Truths to Remember

The Truth Is...

Money does not buy happiness. In fact, the exact opposite may be true.

The Truth Is...

The important things in life cannot be bought.

The Truth Is...

Earthly possessions are temporal.

The Truth Is...

No matter how much money we have, we always want more.

The Truth Is...

God gives us as much money as we can handle.

The Truth Is...

You reap what you sow.

The Truth Is...

The love of money can lead us astray.

I Need a Man to Be Complete

The lie that a girl needs a man to be complete has tripped up many of us. I believed this lie: I thought I needed a man to make me happy and, as a result, wasted years of my life with the wrong type of guys. Watching a romantic comedy, I'd dream of the day when I, too, would fall in love and live happily ever after just like in the movies. I was sure I'd meet a gorgeous, rich man who would make my life complete.

But dating several men and having four serious relationships taught me that falling in love can be painful and devastating. When the one I loved didn't love me back, my spirit was crushed by the rejection. Still, I kept believing that somehow that perfect man would find me and sweep me off my feet. Well, a handful of different men did sweep me off my feet—and then drop-kicked me into a ditch! Men who used lies and manipulation to get what they wanted and then left me hurting and alone caused me to hate all men with a frighteningly intense passion.

The truth is, I didn't need a man in my life to complete me. I needed a savior. I needed *the* Savior. I needed Jesus, and He saved me from my sorrow, healed my broken heart, and loved me like no man had. Jesus helped me realize that I didn't need a man to make me content. Although God did finally give me a wonderful husband, Jesus Christ remains the love of my life.

Below are some truths I wish I had known when I was dating. Instead, I kept settling for the wrong guy and wasting irreplaceable time.

The Truth Is……

Love is not merely hot passion or lust.

When we girls first meet a guy we like, we experience a rush of oxytocin, that wonderful feel-good hormone that makes us euphoric and increases our physical attraction toward the opposite sex. But this hormone also clouds the brain, making us believe that infatuation and love are the same thing. The hormone also temporarily blinds us to the other person's faults, causing us to only notice the positive things about the guy and how crazy in love we are.

In **1 Corinthians 13:4-8** God gives us this description of genuine love:

> *Love endures long and is patient and kind.*
> *Love never is envious nor boils over with jealousy.*
> *Love is not boastful or vainglorious.*
> *Love does not display itself haughtily.*
> *Love is not conceited (arrogant and inflated with pride).*
> *Love is not rude (unmannerly) and does not act unbecomingly.*
> *Love (God's love in us) does not insist on its own rights or its own way.*
> *Love is not self-seeking.*
> *Love is not touchy or fretful or resentful.*
> *Love takes no account of the evil done to it (it pays no attention to a suffered wrong).*
> *Love does not rejoice at injustice and unrighteousness, but rejoices when right and truth prevail.*
> *Love bears up under anything and everything that comes.*
> *Love is ever ready to believe the best of every person; it hopes are fadeless under all circumstances, and it endures everything (without weakening).*
> *Love never fails (never fades out or becomes obsolete or comes to an end).*

When I first read this passage, I was shocked to see no mention of physical intimacy! I thought love was all about the physical attraction, about hot passion for the opposite sex. Boy, was I wrong! In this passage of Scripture, God teaches us how to treat people we love. This is very important to know in any relationship but especially when you're looking for a spouse.

Besides, how can we recognize true love if we don't understand what love is or know what it looks like?

Surprisingly, true love between a man and a woman isn't the roller-coaster, passionate, exciting feeling we experience early on in a relationship. Don't allow your fleshly lusts to lead you into wrong relationships—as I did far too many times. Despite what Hollywood suggests, that heat burns out eventually, but if someone really loves us, the embers stay warm and alive.

Make your desire for a spouse a topic of prayer and let the Lord guide you. Also ask Him to help you keep your eyes open when you meet someone interesting. Remember that a person's actions speak louder than words. A guy can say he loves you, but does he act like it? Let **1 Corinthians 13:4-8** help you answer that question. Keep the following truths in mind as well.

The Truth Is......
It is best to date men who have the same beliefs as you.

> ***Do not be unequally yoked with unbelievers [do not make mismated alliances with them or come under a different yoke with them, inconsistent with your faith]. For what partnership have right living and right standing with God with iniquity and lawlessness? Or how can light have fellowship with darkness?***
> *— 2 Corinthians 6:14*

In this verse, God warns Christians not to "be unequally yoked with unbelievers." As God's light on this dark planet, we are to be friendly to everyone, but we are not to develop a close romantic friendship with a man who does not have the same beliefs that we do. Spending time with a person who doesn't share your moral values or your Christian faith means you two are heading in two totally different directions in life. It is far more beneficial to you to obey God and hang out with someone who is heading down the same road you are: you'll also encounter fewer obstacles and conflicts of interests. Also, remember that the main reason we date is to find a mate to share our lives with. So why would you want to date someone who doesn't believe what you believe?

After enough heartache, after enough wandering through life in pursuit of a wealthy man to marry, I chose to make my relationship with God my top priority. My heart had been broken to pieces, but I sensed He was putting it back together. So the last thing I wanted was to date a man who thought going to church was stupid. If I were to have a boyfriend, he needed to understand me, not judge me, and absolutely not pull me away from God. For years I had changed who I was in order to attract the opposite sex, and I lost my identity in the process. (Learn from me and ask yourself whether you change for better or for worse when you are around the man you're interested in!) But after my traumatic blind date, I knew to ask God for wisdom about relationships so I wouldn't waste any more time dating a loser.

Another reason to ask God for wisdom is because some guys will say anything to get what they want—and that "anything" includes you. If he suddenly starts attending church when he's never bothered to before or if he suddenly professes faith in Christ but you don't see any change in him, don't naively believe what he says. As I've said before, take time to get to know him. Also, don't be too quick to jump into a relationship with a newborn Christian. Let him grow in his relationship with the Lord. Pray for him, be a friend, but also be wise. Make sure you really know the man before getting into any kind of committed relationship.

In **Matthew 12:33** Jesus said this:

> *"Either make the tree sound (healthy and good), and its fruit sound (healthy and good), or make the tree rotten (diseased and bad), and its fruit rotten (diseased and bad); for the tree is known and recognized and judged by its fruit."*

What does this verse have to do with dating? Well, the guy you are attracted to is like a tree. You need to ask yourself, "What kind of fruit is he producing?" You need to evaluate his character and priorities by looking at his fruit, at how he is living his life. Is the fruit good and healthy, or is it diseased and bad? Noticing the type of fruit he produces will help you determine whether or not he is worth dating. Is he spiritually mature enough for you to invest time in getting to know him better? Will he one day be marriage material? Will he be a responsible father? These are important questions to consider before you get too involved with a man.

If only I had done this exercise when I was getting to know Tony! I would have realized that he was a tree full of disease and saved myself years of abuse. I knew Tony was someone who moved from girl to girl, but I naively hoped he would be different with me. Red flags were waving all around me, but in the warm newness of the relationship, I ignored them and kept hoping for the best. The fact is, the best predictor of a person's future behavior is his past behavior. To think I wanted to marry Tony! What a mistake that would have been! I thank God for getting me out of that relationship.

Don't forget that the main reason to date is to find that special person to share your life with forever. So please, I beg you to take your time and choose wisely. If he isn't marriage material, move on quickly.

The Truth Is...
Marriage is hard work.

Marriage is the start of a new chapter in your life, but this blending of two people's lives—of two personalities—isn't always easy. When I married Jay, I thought we'd never have problems because both of us were Christians. But those initial days and months of marriage were far more difficult than I'd ever imagined them being! Both of us were set in our own particular ways, and both of us brought plenty of baggage into our relationship. Yes, our past and our different personalities impacted our relationship! We had a lot of work to do! For one thing we communicated differently. I sometimes thought, *What planet is Jay from?* I didn't understand why he said or did certain things. It was very frustrating—and I could go on and on about our differences. In fact, I could write a whole book on marriage, but the main thing I want to get across to you now is this: marriage isn't easy, it is hard work!

God warns us about this reality in **1 Corinthians 7: 32-35:**

> *My desire is to have you free from all anxiety and distressing care.*

*The unmarried man is anxious about the things of the Lord —
how he may please the Lord;*

*But the married man is anxious about worldly matters — how
he may please his wife —*

*And he is drawn in diverging directions [his interests are
divided and he is distracted from his devotion to God].*

*And the unmarried woman or girl is concerned and anxious
about the matters of the Lord, how to be wholly separated and
set apart in body and spirit; but the married woman has her
cares [centered] in earthly affairs — how she may please her
husband.*

*Now I say this for your own welfare and profit, not to put [a
halter of] restraint upon you, but to promote what is seemly and
in good order and to secure your undistracted and undivided
devotion to the Lord.*

In this passage, God emphasizes that your relationship with Him is to remain your primary relationship, and He is very open about that fact that when we are married, we have less time to spend with Him.

When I got married, I focused a lot of my time and energy and attention on loving and caring for my spouse. At the same time, I was depending on Jay to meet all my needs. I wanted him to say and do all the right things, to shower me with his unconditional love, and to read my mind in order to know what I needed. But Jay is, after all, only human and therefore totally unable to read minds—mine or anyone else's! In fact, he failed terribly to read mine, and I was failing as a wife as well. I was completely unsuccessful in giving Jay the love and respect he needed. Instead, feeling discouraged, I complained and moaned and groaned about how unhappy I was. But I was learning that God is the only One who can fulfill all my needs. After reading many books on marriage and spending years in marriage counseling, I can tell you that staying married is hard work. And it took me awhile to learn to balance my time with God and my time with Jay.

Here's a fundamental guideline: If the guy in your life is taking all your time away from your relationship with the Lord, you are in trouble. Be careful not to get so involved with a guy that you lose your focus on Jesus.

If God is not the number one priority for both you and the man you're dating, I can guarantee He will not be the number one priority in your marriage. My experience is—and the Bible teaches—that you both need to have a relationship with God to make a marriage work. Without grounding your relationship with each other in the relationship with God each of you has, you will both be discouraged and frustrated by your inability to fulfill each other's needs.

But let's back up. Be aware that your emotions and your hormones can be extremely powerful. Before you know it, you may find yourself deeply attached to a man who isn't good for you. Believe me, I know. My physical attraction to Tony kept me in that unhealthy relationship for two years. The physical bond we shared was a key reason I continued to go back for more abuse. I wish I could go back in time and shake some good sense into myself. Looking back, I should have never gotten physically involved with any man I dated. My parents had always preached no sex before marriage. One reason I didn't listen to their advice was I didn't understand the emotional bond that develops between a man and a woman who sleep together. Besides, most of my friends were sleeping around, so what could be the harm? I came to understand, though, that God designed that bond to exist between a husband and a wife, not between two people who simply feel like making that kind of connection.

The Truth Is…
Sex before marriage has consequences.

I know you've heard about the consequences of being sexually active, but a person who is in love enters the land of denial and thinks she'll never face any of these consequences.

The most obvious consequence of sexual activity is an unplanned pregnancy. A single intimate time can drastically change the course of both the boy's and the girl's lives. Regardless of how the pregnancy ends—in abortion, adoption, marriage, or single parenthood—the event is life changing. I am grateful I didn't become pregnant before I was married to Jay, but many of my friends did. So I saw the indescribable heartache of having an abortion, of dealing with it year after year when the calendar reminded of the birthday of their unborn child. That is a date they will never forget.

Another friend allowed her son to be adopted by a lovely Christian couple. She shared the horrific pain of letting her son go, and she dreams of the day that his adoptive parents will make good on their promise to let him meet his two sisters. If they don't follow through, this mom hopes her son will look for her and find her. Unplanned pregnancy can indeed be a dramatic life-changing event.

Sexually transmitted diseases are another possible consequence of sexual activity. In the movies, people hop in and out of bed with one another, but have you ever seen any of those characters struggling with physical ailments like herpes or AIDS? Well, every day in real life, those diseases and many others are transmitted from one person to another behind closed doors. Admit it. If you had a sexually transmitted disease, are you going to post that information on Facebook? I don't think so. The truth is, people get STDs every day. They just don't talk about it! Most of us say, "Oh, that won't happen to me." Well, hopefully it won't happen to you, but it is happening to many young people every day, some of whom—like you—thought it would never happen to them.

An inevitable consequence of sex outside of marriage—and perhaps the hardest one for me to deal with—is one I didn't anticipate. I'm talking about the emotional and psychological effects of fully giving one's self to another person. When a guy, taking that gift lightly, walks away, his action wounds us in our heart of hearts, and his action will negatively affect our future relationships with men. God designed physical intimacy to be shared in a committed relationship with our husband. Some of you are thinking, "But I'm in love!" Imagine—or perhaps remember—how bad it hurts when the person you love and have shared your whole self with treats you poorly or looks at another girl.

Also be aware of the painful reality that some guys make a game of trying to get a girl into bed. Such a man makes all kinds of promises, says whatever it takes, and sounds truly sincere. In the moment he may even be sincere, but later on, after he got what he wanted, he begins to think about whether he honestly wants to marry the girl he conquered. With the challenge over, he sees her as easy and just not as much fun to be around anymore. He may also say that the commitment feels too high, his freedom is threatened, and he backs out. He never once considers the emotional toll his self-centered actions took on the girl. He's off to find a new challenge!

Again, none of us ever thinks this will happen to us, but every day girls are left brokenhearted and bitter after a relationship with this kind of guy. I know. I was that girl. Angry, I thought all guys were like this, which wasn't true—there still are godly guys out there—but the hurt I experienced took years to heal and made it hard for me to trust men in my later relationships.

So I can't caution you strongly enough to beware of this love-her-and-leave-her guy! He may go back to you, say he realizes how stupid he was, and seem to recommit himself to you and the relationship, but after he sleeps with you again—after he has had his urges met, after playing his little game and winning—he'll usually disappear once again. Why does this happen? Because we girls fall for it! Because we girls allow men to treat us this way! Don't allow yourself to be a victim of this type of abuse.

Imagine for a moment if every single girl in the world always said no to sex before marriage. Guys would probably be way more interested in getting married. Nowadays a man can have his cake and eat it too: he can get the sex he wants *and* keep his freedom. Too many women are putting out, so why would a man want to get married when he can have sex with a different girl every weekend? This is a sad fact. Again, if only we girls could stick together and be strong enough to say no, we would have a serious impact on the way men treated women.

I honestly cringe when I look back at my past, at the abusive boyfriend in high school and the compulsive liar who cheated over and over. As if the scene weren't set for disaster already, I believed that every guy who wanted to sleep with me actually loved me. I didn't deserve any of this kind of treatment, and neither do you. Bottom line, when a boyfriend is in any way physically abusive with you, an alarm should go off in your mind telling you to get out now! And be sure you do exactly that!

The Truth Is...
Abuse is never acceptable, and it tends to escalate.

If a guy ever pushes you or slaps you, he isn't someone you want to date—or marry. The reality is, the abuse will only escalate after marriage. If he verbally insults you, if he puts you down in front of his friends and insists he's just joking, and if when you call him on it he refuses to change his behavior, he is *not* the man for you. Don't waste any more time on him. Get out! Tell a parent or a close friend what is happening and then move on. The abuse will only get worse. As a friend told me, if a guy treats you badly in public, then be afraid of how he will treat you in private! Stop and think for a moment: How does your boyfriend treat you in public?

As you read in the first half of this book, my high-school boyfriend became possessive, demanding, and eventually physically abusive. Yet I believed him each time he said that he was sorry and that he'd change. I even gave up going away to college in order to be with him. I allowed him to control some of my most important life decisions.

Clearly, abusers change who we are, how we think about ourselves, and how we respond to the world. Boyfriends, especially high-school ones, should not have that much influence over us or over any decisions we make. Even in college, when the more serious dating begins, we have to be careful not to allow boyfriends too much say in what we do. And as for the abusive one, who harms you physically in any way at all, get out while you can. If you don't—and this is the ugly truth—one day he may harm you permanently.

One more word on this topic. Girls, we have to be so diligent to protect ourselves. Satan often presents his best to us before God presents *His* best, and since Satan is the deceiver, his stuff can look pretty good. So guard yourself in all your relationships; be careful and prayerful about whom you befriend. Avoid violent men at all costs. Any guy who is cruel to animals or children or who belittles others is not the kind of man you want to share your life with. Choose wisely. Don't be so desperate for a relationship that you make a tragic mistake. It's better to be in no relationship at all than to be in an abusive one. Believe it or not, you can live without a man even though your heart may be saying otherwise.

The Truth Is...
Only God can fulfill all our needs. Men can't.

God is the only One who can supply all our needs, and He is absolutely essential to any successful marriage. Even if we bring very little baggage into a relationship, we can't depend on a guy to fix it. Men can be a blessing, but they tend to come with their own set of problems too.

So realize that if we allow God to direct us, He has a wonderful plan for your life and mine, with or without a guy. God can show us the exact right mate for us, just as He did for me. In His perfect timing and amazing way, God placed me right next door to the man I was to marry. Now you and I may think we want to be married, but only God knows when we are ready for the best match for us. And even the perfect God-chosen mate for us will not meet all of our needs, but he is nevertheless part of God's plan for us.

And let me just say that Jay and I love each other very much, but only One in this world has true love for us. He is God Himself, for **"God is love." (1 John 4:8)**. He is the only One who will complete you. No man on earth can fill that void the way God can. Keep in mind that God loves you like no man could ever love you. Believing the lie that I needed a man to complete me caused me to settle for less than what I deserved: I allowed abusive men to take control of me, pulling me away from Jesus. Remember these truths when a man comes into your life. Is he worth your precious time?

Truths to Remember

The Truth Is... *Love is not hot passion.*
The Truth Is... *It is best to date men who have the same beliefs as you.*
The Truth Is... *Marriage is hard work.*
The Truth Is... *Sex before marriage has consequences.*
The Truth Is... *Abuse is never acceptable, and it tends to escalate.*
The Truth Is... *Only God can fulfill all our needs. Men can't.*

A Closing Thought

I hope and pray that this book and its companion learning journal have prompted you to reevaluate your life and given you helpful guidelines for decisions you'll make in the future. You have only one life, and I hope you don't make the same mistakes I made. I want to leave you with the following verses because this is my prayer for you.

> I pray that out of his glorious riches he may strengthen you with power through his Spirit in your inner being, so that Christ may dwell in your hearts through faith. And I pray that you, being rooted and established in love, may have power, together with all the saints, to grasp how wide and long and high and deep is the love of Christ, and to know this love that surpasses knowledge—that you may be filled to the measure of all the fullness of God. Now to him who is able to do immeasurably more than all we ask or imagine, according to His power that is at work within us, to him be glory in the church and in Christ Jesus throughout all generations, for ever and ever! Amen. —Ephesians 3:16-21 NIV1984

What God has done for me, He can do for you. Remember that He has a wonderful plan for your life and that He does all things beautifully in His time. God can and will change your life for the better if you allow Him to. He is on your side. It's time you believe that it's God you need. He is the only one who can bring you true love and the wholehearted acceptance that you've longed for.

Chrissie Cory

CPSIA information can be obtained at www.ICGtesting.com
Printed in the USA
BVOW011708240113

311501BV00005B/82/P

9 781449 768362